ANOTHER GLIM

Also by Alan Plowright

Plowright Follows Wainwright
Hot-Foot Through The Highlands
A Glimpse of Yorkshire

ANOTHER GLIMPSE OF YORKSHIRE
Alan Plowright

Alan Plowright

Moorfield Press

First published in Great Britain
by
Moorfield Press 1999

Filmset by
Highlight Type Bureau Ltd, Bradford, West Yorkshire
Printed in England by
The Amadeus Press Ltd, Huddersfield, West Yorkshire

A CIP catalogue record for this book is available from the British Library

ISBN 0 9530 1193 3

Cover photograph - Alan Plowright
Colour photographs: Alan Plowright (unless otherwise indicated in
Acknowledgements)

Contents

Acknowledgements

I am greatly indebted to W.R.Mitchell, Richard Whiteley, Brian Close and Ashley Jackson for allowing me to feature them in this book. Acknowledgement is made to Ashley Jackson for the sketches that appear on pages 140 and 141. My sincere thanks to John W. Holroyd for the compilation of the maps and the remaining sketches, also to Derek Rowson for collating the index.

The following people have kindly allowed the use of illustrations.

W.R. Mitchell – page 2, 4, 9, 12, 13, 16, 17, 48, 53, 132 and colour photograph of Barden Tower
F.W.D. Hodgson – page 26
A. Kidson – page 27
A.L. Kemp – page 32
Walter Scott (Bradford) Ltd. – page 44
Yorkshire Television – page 52
Brian Close – page 78, 80, 84, 90, 94, 95
Doris Woolhouse – page 105
B. Fraser – page 108
J. Worsfold – page 114
Ashley Jackson – page 128, 129, 131, 136, 137
Tasker Photographic Trust – page 133
Skipton Castle – page 148
Abbot Hall Art Gallery and Museum, Kendal – page 154, 155
David J. H. Clifford – page 158, 159

Foreword
By Hannah Hauxwell

I met Alan Plowright for the first time when he came to my home for a chat concerning his proposal for me to feature in his book entitled *A Glimpse of Yorkshire*. During our discussion I gave him a resume of my life at Low Birk Hatt and how it compared to that at the cottage where I now reside. We also discussed my lifelong interest in music and poetry, which has resulted in some of the happiest moments of my childhood.

I learned that Alan knew nothing of Yorkshire and its inspiring Dales until he moved to Baildon in the course of his work and became involved in long-distance walking. This activity introduced him to the windswept moorland landscapes and pleasant lowland footpaths of the area. In the course of his travels he grew to admire not only the county's scenic qualities, but also its commendable and forthright inhabitants.

Accounts of his journeys and his meetings with a rich abundance of characters have been subsequently outlined in his books and I was pleased to feature in one of them.

It is a pleasure to recommend his latest compilation, which outlines visits to further diverse locations in Yorkshire and also provides an insight into the lives of another cast of interesting personalities.

Hannah Hauxwell 1999

Introduction

The attributes of Yorkshire are so abundant and varied that I had no difficulty in selecting another collection of diverse locations to feature in this book. Its terrain ranges from the chalk of the undulating Wolds to the limestone of the resplendent Dales and the coal measures of South Yorkshire.

The Wolds is an area that was unknown to me until two years ago when I began exploring their ancient chalk uplands and inviting settlements. A good way to discover the latent charms of this region, which sweeps northwards from the Humber to the foot of the Cleveland Hills, is to sample the Wolds Way. This enriching long–distance path begins within sight of the mighty Humber Bridge and ends at Filey, where it joins the Cleveland Way. The chapter entitled 'A Walk in the Wolds' illustrates a journey from its starting point to the deserted medieval village of Wharram Percy. It is an excursion through some of the richest agricultural land in the county and the rippling hills, riven by deeply carved chalk valleys, provide memorable vistas.

My recent walks through the countryside and towns of South Yorkshire were a remarkable eye-opener. Gone were the disfiguring slag-heaps, pit-head winding gear and belching chimneys. Their replacements are country parks, nature reserves and land that has been returned to its former state. 'The Changing Face of South Yorkshire' reveals the rejuvenated environment of this former heavily industrialised region.

I have always had affection for the quieter Dales and Littondale, one of my favourites, is visited in 'The Enduring Dale.' Its gateway lies just beyond Kilnsey Crag, as you travel through Wharfedale towards Kettlewell. Its lush lowland pastures and limestone flanks form ideal grazing land and it largely escaped the influx of industry that affected parts of the Dales. The River Skirfare meanders through the dale, passing sequestered hamlets in its upper reaches before frolicking beneath the gaze of picturesque Arncliffe church. As it nears the foot of the dale a scattering of ancient farms, two of which are former granges of Fountains Abbey, fleck the landscape. In winter the snow-covered slopes of Horsehead Moor, which ring the head of the dale, form one of the finest vistas of the Dales.

A unique journey through the Dales and onwards to Eden is outlined in 'The Redoubtable Lady.' The title refers to Lady Anne Clifford, who travelled regularly through her estates in North Yorkshire and Westmorland, which she inherited after the Civil War. Her historic 'Trail', as it has become known, is followed from Skipton Castle to Brougham, near Penrith. She spent the latter part of her life restoring her castles at Skipton, Pendragon, Brough, Appleby and Brougham and living in each by turn. Through her charitable works she founded the Hospital of St Anne at Appleby and repaired churches in Appleby, Brougham and Mallerstang.

W.R.Mitchell is a name that is synonymous with the Yorkshire Dales, for he has known them intimately for more than sixty years, initially discovering them as a young journalist. During his extensive career as Editor of *The Dalesman* he has probably had greater contact with dalesfolk than anyone and has become 'The Consummate Dalesman.' His prodigious output of books includes many portrayals of this trustworthy and hardy breed, which vividly depict their humour, cussedness and sincerity. Bill is never lost for a good anecdote and in his retirement he is still busy, writing for 'occupational therapy,' as he describes it.

There can be few people to whom Richard Whiteley is not instantly recognisable. He has the distinction, according to Sir David Frost, of making a record number of appearances on television. His fond memories of childhood in Baildon and his days at Giggleswick School are outlined in 'Countdown to Success.' The latter's traditions and Russell Harty's inspirational teaching are vividly recalled. Yorkshire Television, still in its infancy, provided his first career break, in *Calendar*, which set him on the road to success. The programme with which he has become most widely associated, *Countdown*, remains as popular as ever after seventeen years.

The highly successful career of Yorkshire and England cricketer Brian Close is revealed in 'I took the Blows,' which is a story of all-round sporting talent, determination and a 'will to win.' Renowned for his firmness and expertise as a captain, he motivated and moulded many young players in his care. His honesty and bluntness did not serve him well on occasions and he was the subject of undeserved controversy.

Water colourist Ashley Jackson's early life was one of upheaval and strife. His family brought him to Yorkshire, from Malaya, at the age of ten and he began to put down roots for the first time. His artistic talent was his saving grace but he had to battle for years to become an established and well-respected landscape painter. He is greatly indebted to Ron Darwent, who gave him his first job, as a sign-writer, and it was this skill that provided a vital means of support through the long battle for recognition. 'The Moors are my Mistress' reveals his years of struggle and also the forces that drew him to the wild moorlands where he creates the exciting and atmospheric panoramas for which he is renowned.

Alan Plowright 1999

CHAPTER ONE

The Consummate Dalesman

Very few people will leave such an indelible imprint on the history of the Yorkshire Dales as W.R. (Bill) Mitchell. This friendly, modest man can recall more than half a century of association with the area, which has been, and still remains, his interest and his passion. His feelings for the Dales far surpass the Bradford man, who was taken on a tour of them by his daughter and exclaimed: 'Its nowt but scenery!'

This is an example of the limitless store of anecdotes that Bill enjoys relating and humorous comments such as this are liberally sprinkled throughout multitudes of his articles and books. A prolific author, he even surprised himself when he recently counted his publications and found that he has produced over one hundred. He laughingly tells of the instance when Alfred Wainwright introduced him to someone as the man who writes a book every ten minutes.

Bill was born on the doorstep of the Dales, or to be more precise, at its gateway, for this is how his birthplace, the attractive market town of Skipton is described. He arrived during the depression of the late 1920's, a time of struggle and hardship, but also one of companionship and shared privation.

A 'mill town lad' is how he describes himself. His earliest memories are of an all-embracing slump, when mill chimneys didn't smoke and people had very little money. Saturday pennies were reduced to Saturday halfpennies, as no one had much cash to lavish on spending money.

The resilient community had come to terms with a lack of money. Nobody felt that they were poor because they were all in the same boat. One or two notables, such as Tom Lumb, who was a pillar of the local chapel, were considered extremely wealthy because they lived in large houses.

Bill remembers chapel days, when Tom Lumb noisily produced sweets wrapped in crinkly paper and passed them to those around him, oblivious to the distraction they may have caused. If a service extended beyond an hour Tom would loudly and pointedly cough,

W. R. (Bill) Mitchell

in order to remind the errant preacher that he had gone on for long enough.

Skipton Auction Mart typified the town of his boyhood and gave it a countryfied feel. It emitted the sounds of cattle that blended with the hooter of Dewhirst's Mill. Bill recalls farmers thronging the auction mart and small armies of mill workers blocking the road into town as they hurried to and from work. The rainbow hues of the River Aire, stained by the emissions from the mill dye house, are also etched in his memory.

Dan Binns, the celebrated water colourist, produced a famous painting of the auction mart in 1928, which depicted that focal point of the town exactly as Bill remembers it.

'The Dales came right to Skipton,' is how he describes his initial awareness of them. His embryonic feelings for the countryside were enhanced by a popular radio programme of that era, *Walks with Romany.* It sparked his interest in natural history as he listened religiously, along with thousands of other devotees, to each glorious episode. It was a bitter disappointment however, to discover that the programme, complete with sound effects, was produced in a studio. The stirring sounds of rippling streams and delicate birdsong were derived from shellac records.

The accomplished Kearton brothers of Thwaite were two of his boyhood icons. He read many of the exquisite books written by these sons of a Swaledale gamekeeper, for they figured amongst the early pioneers of wildlife photography. As a young boy he learned of their adventures in the Scottish Highlands and remembers in particular their voyage from Glasgow to the remote island of St. Kilda, where they lived for a period in order to study the indigenous sea birds. The sights and sounds of the island were vividly brought to life in their descriptions of the sea pounding the mighty cliffs and the evocative calls emanating from the bird colonies. They also told stories of the resolute inhabitants, most of who had never visited the mainland.

Bill was determined to visit St. Kilda, a dream that was finally accomplished fifty years later, following his retirement from the Dalesman Publishing Company. He went with a party from the National Trust for Scotland and spent two inspiring weeks on the island. The expedition gave rise to two of his many books, *Voyage to the Edge of the World* and a study of Finlay MacQueen, one of the local patriarchs.

David Pearson of Langstrothdale

At the age of fifteen Bill left school to begin a journalistic career that was to span fifty years. He became a novice reporter with the *Craven Herald*, the Skipton based newspaper, which was instrumental in his introduction to the Yorkshire Dales. His early career was very similar to that of Luke Casey, the popular presenter of Yorkshire Television's *Dales Diary*, who began his working life as a fledgling reporter with the *Northern Echo*, based in Darlington. Luke's early assignments introduced him to the attractions of the North York Moors, where he revelled in his access to the striking heather-clad moorland and picturesque villages of the Cleveland Hills.

Correspondingly, Bill's forays took him to all parts of the Dales and introduced him to its inimitable inhabitants. For his pains he received the princely sum of 12s.6d.a week. He counted himself lucky, for he was the first 'cub' reporter ever to be given a wage. Travel was by bus, train or 'Shanks's pony' and he recalls walking with a fellow journalist from Grassington to Kettlewell, to attend the funeral of C.J. Cutcliffe Hyne, the Bradford author and creator of 'Captain Kettle.' Although such outings were often strenuous, Bill was happy to experience the Dales in the best possible way.

He recalls meeting an elderly man, with a lively tread, on one of his excursions. Announcing that he was well into his eighties, the man remarked: 'When this pace stops, I stops.'

The Second World War was still in progress during his early years at the *Craven Herald*. He can still recall the rumble of tanks as they ploughed along Skipton High Street and the drone of enemy aircraft bound for Liverpool. Richard Greene, the film star, famous for his role as Robin Hood, was based in the town in a different capacity, as an army officer. Bill can also remember the P.O.W. camp, beside the road to Bolton Abbey, inhabited by Italians and then Germans. They were frequently seen, on parole, walking around the town in shabby battledress, with conspicuous orange or yellow patches on the backs of their tunics.

On his first morning as a journalist, Bill was introduced to Harry Scott, the originator of *The Yorkshire Dalesman*, forerunner of the *Dalesman*. Harry was the first real journalist that he had met and he was astonished to be greeted by a quotation from Shakespeare and hailed as 'blithe spirit.' It was mid-morning and Harry had arrived just in time for coffee and one of Mr. Bean's succulent pork pies. He had founded his monthly magazine just before the outbreak of war, whose conditions unfortunately froze its circulation at 4,000, necessitating his acceptance of a part-time job at the *Herald* to augment the family income.

Harry did not fit the mould of hard-bitten reporters; in fact he was the most amiable of men and Bill never saw him lose his temper. He had a mischievous sense of humour, a quick wit and an inspiring way with words. The reporters' room was frequently filled with the fall-out from his beloved pipe, which he crammed with Tom Long tobacco. He would puff away to his heart's content whilst scribbling copious amounts of copy with a soft pencil, a throwback to his time as leader-writer on the *Yorkshire Post*.

In 1935 Harry had moved to a 'little house,' as it was advertised in a newspaper, at Clapham. It stood on the Ingleborough Estate owned by the Farrer family and is, in fact, the imposing 'Fellside,' which is still one of the village's landmarks. This is where *The Yorkshire Dalesman* began its life in 1939, and at that time it was the only monthly magazine of its kind in the county. The house was later to feature significantly in Bill's life, but not until he had done his stint of National Service.

Bill joined the Royal Navy in 1946 and served the normal requirement of two years. His initial posting was to HMS Royal Arthur, which turned out to be Butlin's Holiday Camp at Skegness. All naval bases bear the names of ships and the appropriate parlance and procedures are observed, including a system of watches. Bill remembers spending one of the night watches marching up and down outside the toilet block.

Another phase of his training involved 'boat pulling' and this was carried out at Malvern. He also spent much of the time sprinting around the picturesque Malvern Hills that have distinct associations with the notable composer, Sir Edward Elgar. Little did Bill realise that one day he would carry out exhaustive research into Elgar's connections with the Yorkshire Dales.

Bill recalls an episode whilst at a naval camp by the York road at Wetherby. With a friend he capsized whilst canoeing on the River Wharfe, embarrassingly in naval uniform, under the gaze of amused onlookers.

After training, his next destination was Ford, an air station in Sussex. Here he was employed, according to his own description, as a 'humble store-basher.'

The next posting, to HMS Fieldfare, at Everton, near the Cromarty Firth, turned out to be a revelation. This glorious setting was a bird-watcher's paradise, frequented by a variety of species. When the runway at the base was not being used by a postwar accumulation of clapped out aircraft, it was commandeered by flocks of golden plover and geese. Sunderland flying boats used the adjacent Firth and when they were absent their replacements were some graceful swans.

Another transfer followed, this time to HMS Gannet, at Eglinton, near Londonderry, in Northern Ireland. Bill found this posting fascinating for he was able to explore neighbouring Donegal on a service bicycle. This charming area lies across the border and servicemen were not allowed to cross it wearing naval uniform. To get round this restriction, common practice was to unpick badges from their attire, to avoid identification. There was nothing in Irish regulations, however, regarding the use of naval bicycles that clearly displayed revealing numbers and advantage was taken of this oversight.

Skipton High Street

View from Giggleswick Scar

Prior Moon's Bridge Malham

Clapham

It was on the towering cliffs of Donegal that Bill encountered the sea birds that became an enduring interest. He was captivated by the colonies of puffins, razorbills and guillemots that inhabited the majestic coastline.

The name of that particular base gave rise to considerable humour and embarrassment, because in naval parlance, 'gannet' describes someone who eats too much. Some unfortunate matelots had to display 'HMS Gannet' on their caps, but Bill was spared this indignity, for he wore a 'fore and aft' uniform, which included a single-breasted tunic and a peaked cap.

On his return to 'civvy street,' Bill received a letter from Harry Scott, inviting him to Fellside, 'to talk over several possibilities.' Shortly afterwards an orange-sided 'Pennine' bus delivered him to Clapham on a trip diced with adventure. In those days the roads presented much more of a challenge than their modern counterparts. He stared with disbelief at *Ye Olde Naked Man*, a café in Settle, and hung on to the seat in front as the valiant bus tangled with Buckhaw Brow. The nonchalant driver kept the vehicle on the road by grasping the steering wheel with one hand whilst his other groped for, located and delivered to his eager mouth some succulent bacon butties.

During the journey Bill encountered his first pot-holer, a young man who clambered on to the bus with a rope ladder coiled around him. An old lady asked if he was 'one o' them pot-hoiler chaps.' He nodded. Her next question stumped him. 'Doesn't ta think tha'll spend enuff time under t'ground wi'out going there now?'

As the bus approached Clapham a flat-topped hill dominated the skyline and an old farmer seated nearby remarked: 'That's Ingleborough ...It's a big rough hill, where t'wind's strong enuff to blaw a sheep o'er.' Bill stared in awe at one of the most distinctive and wildest fells in the Dales.

In those days all traffic ground its way through Clapham. A large vehicle, carrying a cargo of tinned food, then subject to rationing, had failed to negotiate a difficult corner and descended into Fell Beck. What had been for centuries a peaceful, law-abiding community, suddenly changed to one of wreckers. Every household, including that of the village constable, who was laid low with sciatica, had a share of the contraband, but they were presented with a problem. The water had washed away the labels

'Fellside', Clapham

and the miscreants were faced with Russian roulette whenever they prepared a meal.

The outcome of Bill's discussion with Harry Scott was that he became one half of the editorial staff of *The Dalesman*, whose magazine circulation had more than trebled since wartime. He moved into lodgings in Clapham, a village that looked ancient, but in reality was of nineteenth-century vintage

The old Clapham was re-styled by the Farrer family who had lived in style at Ingleborough Hall. A number of tunnels were provided for tradesfolk and others to reach the back door of the hall. Clapdale Lake was created to provide a water supply. It was

'High Dale Country' – Barns in Swaledale

also stocked with fish to indulge the family's preference for angling.

Shortly after the end of the war the hall was sold and converted to a special school, owned by the West Riding County Council, where children suffering from chest ailments could benefit from fresh air and exercise.

Bill tackled his new job with gusto. 'Living by the pen,' as he calls it, he set himself the task of recording Dales life from those who had first hand experience of it. Folk tales, he feels, are of major importance and need preserving, for few written records are in existence. Multitudes of dalesfolk were visited and Bill listened intently to their humorous anecdotes and wry observations. These he has since incorporated into his many publications.

In Bill's words, it was an age of innocence, typified by the tale of the farmer who asked a friend what he thought of 'all this pornography.' His friend replied: 'Nay – I don't know, I haven't got a pornograph.'

He met many notable and interesting characters as he roamed the Dales, his outings conveniently providing access to all parts of them. He recalls an early expedition to Littondale, reaching the dalehead by bus. He was not so lucky on his return, for there were no buses available and he had to walk all the way to Grassington. However, Bill viewed the situation as seeing the Dales in the best possible way.

On another visit to Littondale he remembers walking down the valley feeling the rain and the raw wind. Eventually a lorry pulled up beside him and the driver shouted: 'Tha' can either get in t' cab, on t' back, or on t' running board.' In the cab were three farmers and two dogs. On the back was a steaming load of manure, so Bill chose the running board. He was conveyed down the dale feeling like a member of Scott of the Antarctic's intrepid team and arrived in Grassington on the verge of hypothermia. Staggering from the vehicle, limbs stiff as boards, he had to stomp around for several minutes before circulation was restored.

Other memories of Littondale include walking expeditions in his off-duty hours when he would park his car in Halton Gill and climb to the Horsehead Pass. Here Bill would cut off from the path, walk along the summit ridge and drop down to the Queen's Arms at Litton, where he could enjoy a manly portion of rabbit pie. He once asked a Dales landlord where he got his rabbits from and his host replied: 'Yon hillside o'er there.'

The mother of his friend, Ralph Hannam, ran the Queen's Arms at one time. Ralph was born in the dale. He was one of two brothers who grew up there and went to Skipton Grammar School. After joining the army, Ralph served in Iceland, married a local girl and remained there. Bill made two memorable visits to his friend's house, which lies in a typically Icelandic setting and as soon as you enter, seemingly returns you to the Yorkshire Dales. The walls are covered with water-colour scenes of Wharfedale and Littondale.

During his first outing to Upper Wharfedale, Bill was entranced by this quiet area, where time seemed to stand still. He waved to a farmhand who cycled by, wearing a 'back-can' containing milk drawn from cattle lodged at an outbarn. A roadman was using a sickle to trim the roadside verges amidst a landscape into which no sound penetrated. He met a villager who told him a tale regarding a man, who, when asked when a neighbour had died, replied: 'If she'd lived till tomorrow, she'd have been dead a fortnight.' It appears that her death had occurred at a whist drive. 'It was all very sad,' he continued, 'she had a good hand.'

In Bill's early days at Clapham, he frequently walked through Clapdale to Ingleborough Cave, whose great mouth gave the impression that the limestone cliff, into which it burrowed, was yawning. Here, Arnold Brown, the cave guide, would hand him a candleholder with three prongs and lead him into the show-cave. By the light of Arnold's paraffin lamp and Bill's flickering candles, they would penetrate towards the heart of the cave, passing impressive calcite formations. Arnold tapped many stalactites with the key to the cave-door as they progressed, producing eerie, ringing sounds. One of the most imposing stalactites was known as the 'Sword of Damocles.'

In time, Dorothy Scott, Harry's patient and kind-hearted wife felt that the office should be moved so that she could recover her sitting room. Ingleborough Estate, which had made Fellside available, offered for sale some workshops, 'up t'ginnel,'nearby. These were acquired and extensive rebuilding took place.

On the day that the furnishings and records were transferred, a stiff breeze was blowing. A handcart was borrowed from the estate and piled with papers and small items of office equipment. The cart had barely reached the gate of Fellside when a gust of wind snatched many of the papers and deposited most of them in Fell Beck. Some were retrieved, but several literary masterpieces were carried away in the mischievous beck.

Adjacent to the new office was a large garden, owned by the vicar, who did not enjoy good health and detested gardening. It was surrounded by high walls and had the air of a peaceful monastery garden. This peace was soon shattered because most of it, along with half of an old barn, was purchased by *The Dalesman* to provide more space for the business. Their portion of the barn, where a vicar

The Auction Mart, Hawes

of old had kept his horse and trap, was converted into the editorial office and the garden became a car park.

During his travels around the Dales, Bill has met many notable characters and also hosts of ordinary dalesfolk, in which he has an abiding interest. He is particularly fond of the hardy people who inhabit the more remote dales, for he feels that they are sufficiently isolated to keep their strong Dales characteristics. When conversing with such people, Bill senses their keen sense of identity and tradition.

James Herriot had similar affections for dalesfolk, contending that the further up the dale you went, the more unique and nicer were the people. Alf Wight, as he was in real life, came in and out of Bill's life at *The Dalesman* over a lengthy period, usually by letter, occasionally by telephone and, on two occasions, face to face. He found Alf to be a quiet-spoken, affable man, whose descriptions of Dales life and its people were incredibly precise and accurate.

Bill features the following description, by Alf, of a Dales kitchen, in *Summat and Nowt*, one of his latest books. 'The kitchen was a

Filming cheese-making at Hawes

big flagged place. Enormous. You couldn't help but feel sorry for the women who had to work in such a cold, draughty place. The farmer's wife who opened the door might have an apron made of sacking. Sometimes she had clogs on her feet. Huge sides of fat bacon hung from hooks driven into the ceiling. You had to duck your head to avoid brushing against them. Bacon was what they lived on. Every time you went into a kitchen, there was this lovely smell of bacon being cooked.'

One of Bill's greatest sources of information, regarding life in the Dales, was William Alderson J.P. a farmer from Angram, near Thwaite, in Swaledale. He was widely known as 'Bill up t'steps' and though his former dwelling is now derelict, the steps can still be discerned.

Another character, whom Bill met at Keld, a neighbouring village in Swaledale, is Laurie Rukin, who sang with the Swaledale Singers. His father took the mail up to lonely Tan Hill, the highest pub in England, at the time when it was delivered on foot. Laurie occasionally attends the Sunday morning service at the Methodist chapel in Settle, for a 'good sing,' as he describes it.

Bill mourns the passing of many of the chapels in the Dales, which, he feels, provided communities with a focal point and a sense of values. He was a lay preacher for forty years and has first-hand experience of many of the communal places of worship. During his early days as a Methodist preacher, he had an amusing interlude at Bentham chapel, near Clapham. He was making final preparations for the service when a local farmer, who was a steward of the chapel, asked: 'Is t'a feeling nervous?' Bill replied that he was. 'Nay lad,' quipped the farmer, 'we should be more frightened o' thee, than thou is of us.'

When the opportunity arose to visit Thomas Armstrong, the Swaledale author, at his home, Lawn House, in Low Row, Bill jumped at the chance. Having heard so much about lead-mining, he was keen to meet the creator of *Adam Brunskill,* one of a series of books that had become best-sellers, and which was based on exhaustive research into the local quest for lead. Another of his popular novels, concerning the West Riding textile trade, is *The Crowthers of Bankdam,* one of my particular favourites.

In the drawing room at Lawn House, Bill chatted with Thomas, amidst an array of bookshelves and Dales water-colours, painted by Fred Lawson, the Wensleydale artist. The author, an 'off-cum'd un,' had found that Swaledale folk are slow to accept a stranger. 'They weigh you up carefully. If you get through twelve months and they decide you are all right, you become one of them.' This demonstrates the time-honoured Dales process of 'wintering and summering and wintering again.'

Another memory that Bill cherishes is attending J.B. Priestley's funeral and interment at St. Michael's Church, Hubberholme. The weather on the day of J.B.'s funeral was cold and clammy, causing a local farmer to exclaim: 'T'day looks as if its bin up all neet.'

This tiny place of worship, sequestered in the folds of upper Wharfedale, contains one of only two remaining oak rood lofts in Yorkshire. An exquisitely carved feature, over 500 years old, it compliments the shapely pews, made by Robert ('Mousey') Thompson, of Kilburn, each bearing his trademark, a wooden mouse.

Alfred Wainwright was responsible for one of the truly exciting moments at *The Dalesman,* in Clapham, when Harry Firth, their printer arrived from Kendal bearing a meticulously illustrated book which had been entirely hand-written and hand-drawn. It was the first of what were to become Wainwright's celebrated pictorial guides to the Lake District. He insisted that the book should be printed exactly as it was written, with not a line of type. Bill was allowed to print selected pages from this and successive books in *Dalesman,* by way of publicity.

On their first meeting, which was by appointment, he had agreed to be interviewed, but this never materialised. He looked affable, whenever he emerged from a fog of pipe-smoke, but he cleverly avoided answering Bill's questions. Concluding that he did not wish to be interviewed, Bill realised that he was a very private and shy man. Many years passed before Wainwright overcame his natural shyness and became a well-known media personality.

The two men met occasionally during the succeeding years and often, Wainwright would send a brief typed letter, signed in green ink, which was his trademark. The signature was initially 'A. Wainwright,' but this was eventually reduced to 'AW,' as a sign of friendship.

During their meetings, Bill discovered Wainwright's love of the Dales, which was clearly demonstrated in his *Walks in Limestone Country,* published in 1970. He always had a great respect for the area, particularly Settle, which he described as 'the heart of limestone country.'

Following Wainwright's death in 1991, Bill wrote a tribute to the great man entitled *After You, Mr. Wainwright,* which concerns a small group of admirers who followed in his footsteps. Suffering from 'Wainwrightosis,' Bill and his three friends had climbed many of the Lakeland fells immortalised in AW's guides and this book is an account of their experiences. One of Bill's proudest achievements, during his extensive walking career, is climbing all the 'Wainwright's' in the Lake District, of which there are more than 200. After several years of sweat and toil, he completed the final peak, Lingmell, that casts its great shadow over Wasdale Head, one of the most evocative locations in Lakeland.

Wainwright wrote a foreword for Bill's book, amusingly titled, *It's a long way to MUCKLE FLUGGA.* The following passage forms a warm tribute, which AW did not bestow lightly. 'Bill Mitchell has been a journalist of consistent excellence throughout his working

William Jake in stained glass at Hubberholme Church

life, with an outstanding talent for research and description that established him as a leading literary figure in the north of England. When he became Editor of two popular monthly magazines, *Dalesman* and *Cumbria*, he continued to contribute articles and books on the life and landscapes of the Yorkshire Dales and the Lake District with an occasional foray over the border.

He has had a love affair with the remote places of the Highlands and Islands of Scotland, travelling not as a tourist but as a nomadic wanderer inspired by a special interest in the ornithology and the flora and fauna of these lonely regions.'

The title of the book relates to a short, rocky ridge that protrudes 200 feet above a restless sea and forms the most northerly point of the Shetland Islands and Britain. Bill and his friends began exploring regions of the Scottish Highlands, laughing their way from glen to glen, cracking jokes about wild haggis and waging war against sheep ticks. They harboured a vague notion of eventually reaching the remote outpost of Muckle Flugga, that Bill had seen in a television programme devised and narrated by John Betjeman,

A Victorian print of Giggleswick Church

entitled *A Bird's-eye View of Britain*. Long after the credits had rolled at the end of the exciting episode, he sat thinking of the Flugga, thrilling to its remote setting on the north-west tip of Europe.

The friends' ambition was realised when they finally reached Unst, the most northerly of the Shetland Islands and gazed spellbound at the rocky bastion, which lies just offshore. It was the culmination of their dreams.

Another of Bill's passions concerns Sir Edward Elgar, the subject of one of his many research schemes. He was surprised to learn that Elgar had been to Giggleswick. The reason for his visits to the village where Bill now resides was to see his friend, a local medical practitioner, Charles William Buck. The two had met, as young men, at a BMA gathering in Worcestershire, where Elgar had been asked to entertain the conference delegates. At that time, the budding composer was conductor of a local asylum orchestra and he was required to find extra players for the function. Dr. Buck took his cello and played in the orchestra. He and Elgar got along very well and became firm friends. A bond was established that would last for fifty years.

Bill's research led to a wonderful experience in the Lake District, when he visited the home of Dr. Buck's daughter, Monica. When asked if she had any memorabilia, Monica said that the seat on which Bill was sitting had been given to her father. She then handed over a box of letters that were sent from Elgar to Dr. Buck. Bill was thrilled to see them.

Some years later, Monica died: he received an invitation from a beneficiary to collect some items of interest, books etc. which had belonged to the doctor. In the front room of the house Bill was shown a long-case clock without the working parts. Inside the casing he found a mass of sheet music, some hand written and some printed. These were pieces that Elgar had written during his early visits to Dr. Buck in the 1880's. Some of them were signed 'E of Giggleswyck,' the corruption of the name being one of the composer's fads. Much to Bill's delight he was given these treasures, of which he retains copies. The originals were gifted to the Elgar Foundation, who manage the Elgar Birthplace Museum at Malvern, where Bill was posted during his National Service. It was a very satisfying gesture for him, on two counts. Firstly, he knew that the original scores would be kept in carefully controlled conditions and secondly the copies would ensure that part of Yorkshire's heritage would not be lost.

This happy occurrence marked the culmination of several years of study, not only of the man, but also of his works. Elgar's music ran through Bill's mind to such a degree that he felt drained of emotion and everything else appeared ordinary and mundane by comparison. He looks back on it as a wonderful experience, but it took a year or two before he fully recovered.

Amongst the tales that Bill loves to relate is one concerning his wife's ancestors. Bill and Freda were married at a small church in East Marton, near to her home, a farm at West Marton. A 'Silver Star' bus was hired to transport their relatives and wedding guests from Skipton to the church and afterwards to the reception. All were then conveyed to the bride's home in the countryside and eventually back to Skipton. The hire charge for the bus was a mere £5 for the day.

Freda comes from a farming family, the Bushbys, who lived at Kettlewell. They were related to the Bells, whose lengthy lineage has swelled many a Dales churchyard. Her great-grandmother, with the beguiling name of Isabella Bell, was as tough as nails. She had to bring up a family in the days when many a farmer's wife relied on 'porridge and mouse-muck,' as the old saying goes.

To supplement the family budget, she rode a horse over Fleet Moss, the highest road in the Dales, to buy two piglets at the market in Hawes. They were then reared, largely on household scraps, at virtually no cost. When the fattened pigs were slaughtered, the meat from one of them was kept to feed the family and that of the other was taken to Hawes to be sold. The money from the sale was used to buy two more piglets and so the cycle began once more.

Another of Freda's ancestors was converted to the Mormon faith. He left his native dale and headed for Liverpool with his wife. They crossed the Atlantic by sailing ship and disembarked at the meeting of the Missouri and Mississippi Rivers. A harrowing journey through 'Indian country' followed, with the husband employed as one of the men in charge of a wagon train. After this spell in the 'wild west,' they arrived in Salt Lake City, at the time when it was just being established.

Letters relating to that perilous journey and their life in Salt Lake City were passed down through the generations of the family. Bill gave the letters to the Mormon Church and its members were thrilled to receive such a unique account of their embryonic headquarters.

In addition to compiling his many books Bill was kept busy with the editing of *Dalesman* and *Cumbria* and, for a time, *Pennine* magazine, now *Peak and Pennine*. He worked diligently on these and the numerous articles that he has contributed to other publications.

Throughout those years he kept up his love affair with the Dales, particularly its friendly and resourceful inhabitants. He declares that every dale is different and each one retains its individual character. For instance, his view of Swaledale, which has always appealed strongly to him, is one of contrast, in some respects beautiful, in others an eyesore. He does not mean that the latter, caused by the remnants of lead-mining on its higher reaches, is necessarily bad. He believes that the whole dale has a certain charm and there is a kind of rightness about the existence of the mines. They add character to the dale.

In 1987 Bill retired from *The Dalesman,* having given thirty-nine years faithful service. He has spent twenty of those enjoyable years as Editor and after relinquishing that post he is able to stay at home and concentrate on writing 'good quality rubbish,' as he humorously describes it.

He now holds the honorary title of Editorial Advisor to *The Dalesman* and still contributes regularly to its magazines. In his early *Dalesman* years, Bill had written leading articles for the *Craven Herald,* where he began his long career. Times have changed, however, since its editorials of those early days, which addressed such momentous issues as drystone walls, litter and the extortionate increase in a farm labourer's wage, when it rose to £3 a week.

Bill's outstanding service to north-country journalism and to the community has been acknowledged by the award, two years ago, of the MBE. Typical of his generous nature is the fact that he was one of the first to congratulate Ian Dewhirst, the Keighley lecturer and historian, who recently received the same award.

The University of Bradford conferred upon him an honorary degree of Doctor of Letters and he also holds honorary membership of the Yorkshire Dales Society.

Not bad for a mill town lad!

CHAPTER TWO
A Walk in the Wolds

A band of chalk covers a substantial portion of East Yorkshire. It stretches northwards from the Humber, almost to the foot of the North York Moors. This area, known as the Wolds, is an extensive tract of rolling countryside that gives a unique character to the East Riding. Its wave-like landscape is cleaved with shapely valleys, their steeply angled sides almost isometric. This bucking, roller coaster of arable land is clothed with brown furrows, waving cereal crops and green hedgerows that range to distant horizons.

Until the eighteenth century it remained barren and unfettered, fit only for hardy sheep. The chief architects of its transformation were the Sykes family, of Sledmere House, who enclosed, cultivated and tended around 1400 square miles of it.

Its western boundary exhibits a range of white ridges to those approaching from York and Selby. They signify the graveyard of innumerable plankton, a land formed by millions of tiny organisms that were deposited on pre-historic sea-beds. The essence of chalk is a landscape folded into the creases of the mind, where everything is promised, semi-obscured and understated. Daniel Defoe described chalklands as the 'fine carpet-ground of England, soft as velvet and the herbage sweet as garden herbs underfoot.' It was also contended in those times that the flesh of the sheep that grazed the land was already flavoured with thyme before they reached the butcher's shop.

Most chalk is too soft for building purposes, but some, extracted from closely compacted layers in the Wolds, has been used in the construction of houses and cottages that adorn its rich variety of villages. Chalk has, however, been extensively used internally, one fine example being the vaults in Westminster Abbey. It is said that migrating birds make use of chalk ridges as a navigational aid, by following them on their extensive flights.

Through this pleasant countryside winds the Wolds Way, a rewarding long-distance footpath that begins in the shadow of the Humber Bridge and terminates seventy-nine miles away on the cliffs above Filey. In this particular chapter, a section of the route will be followed from its starting point to the deserted medieval village of Wharram Percy that lies near Sledmere.

An inscribed stone marks its commencement at Hessle, on the banks of the Humber. The initial section of the path follows the north bank and passes a small country park that provides a rural contrast to the concrete expanse of the Humber Bridge. Along the river bank fishermen huddle, lines awaiting response from the assortment of fish that have thankfully returned to the river; a tribute to the pollution control of recent years.

The Way soon turns north heading for Welton, where the chalk of the Wolds meets the clay of the Humber estuary. The foot of Welton Dale marks the entry into the Wolds landscape. This dale is thankfully secreted from the nearby A63 trunk road, which scythes through the area heading for Hull, and a delightful stretch of walking unfolds as the path is followed through its wooded glades. Within this tranquil vale a series of springs gurgle amidst entwining undergrowth and feed a lengthy pond that lies on the outskirts of Welton. Such ponds are a familiar feature of Wolds villages, often frequented by families of ducks and the occasional geese.

A stream progresses from here into the centre of the village through a narrow ornamental channel, spanned by a tiny stone footbridge. This delightful watercourse soon broadens into another pond, surrounded by graceful willows, their arching boughs forming shapely emerald domes. The pleasing scene lies under the gaze of the imposing tower and decorative west front of the parish church.

Nearby lies the inviting village green, surrounded by a bevy of attractive eighteenth and nineteenth-century buildings, displaying tasteful frontages of dusky brick beneath the brighter reds of their pantile roofs. Set amongst these is the agreeable Green Dragon Inn that offers hospitality and refreshment in a relaxing setting. This attractive, white walled hostelry is reputed to be the former haunt of John Palmer, alias Dick Turpin, and the place where he was eventually captured.

An unconventional fountain occupies pride of place in the centre of The Green, as it is known. This round edifice, built of weathered stone, has stood here for over 200 years and it is topped with ornately carved panels that support a curvaceous dome. A

Humber Bridge – start of the Wolds Way

The Green, Welton

A Wolds valley

Wharram Percy

small spout protrudes near its base, but no water appears to issue from it. Despite its seeming lack of purpose it is easy on the eye, particularly in spring when it is surrounded by the golden glow of daffodils that enliven The Green.

The fountain has connections with a previous vicar of Welton who moved here in 1787, to take charge of the church, which had been carefully restored more than a century earlier. His daughter is responsible for the erection of the memorial fountain.

Within sight of The Green stand two late eighteenth-century dwellings, Welton Hall and Welton Manor. Secreted behind a high wall is Welton Grange, an older, stone-built property, which was constructed for a Hull merchant who made his fortune in maritime trade.

Beyond the village, Welton Dale immediately demonstrates the typical characteristics of a Wolds valley. A gentle, grassy gorge is a fitting description. Its steep, regularly proportioned sides cocoon the traveller from the surrounding countryside and create a feeling of immunity from the outside world. The flat valley floor is mainly coated with lush grassland, but in places pine and birch woods line it. On its crests lie wind breaks of hawthorn and beech and gorse intrudes onto its protective sides.

Emerging from Welton Dale, the Wolds Way soon changes direction and heads west towards the village of Brantingham, where it once again comes perilously close to the busy trunk road, the A63. It veers north on the outskirts of Brantingham just in time to avoid contact with the artery that links the port of Hull with the M62 motorway and the towns and cities of the West Riding.

Although the Way skirts the pleasant hamlet, it is worth a short detour. Typical of many Wolds settlements, it displays an endearing mixture of old and new. The pristine facades of modern buildings mingle with the rustic brick and yellow stone of mellow cottages, enhanced by wooden porches. Its undisturbed rural atmosphere possesses a sense of timeless beauty; typified by Brantingham Hall, a tall, stately building which overlooks the village pond. Slim of build and fronted with a multitude of windows, it is a fine example of eighteenth-century workmanship.

A complete contrast is provided by the Gothic war memorial, constructed with stone taken from Hull's Town Hall of 1862.

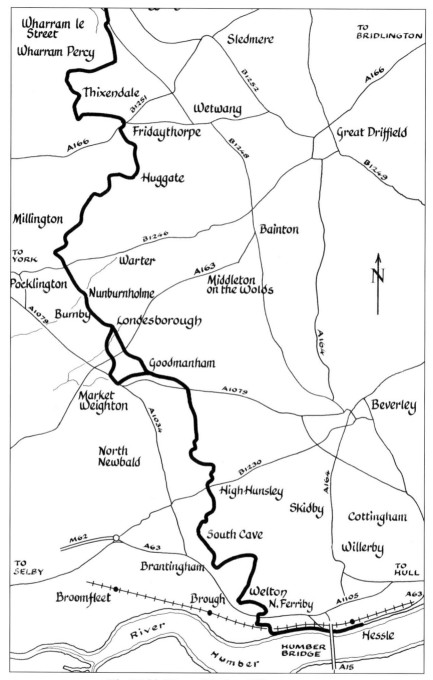

The Wolds Way – Hessle to Wharram Percy

Pevsner describes it as 'lovably awful,' and it must be conceded that its designer had an off day. Full of good intentions, it is a curious architectural mixture. Its most striking feature is the collection of marble pillars that both surround and crown it. Each pillar is topped with a round tapered headstone, which creates the vision of a group of missiles, fitted with warheads, awaiting blast-off.

Secreted on the edge of the village stands Thorpe Hall, dating from the sixteenth century and rebuilt during the Victorian period. It is claimed that from its impressive gardens and lawns, the twin landmarks of Lincoln Cathedral and York Minster can be seen.

A short section of road walking is required as the Way leaves the vicinity of Brantingham, passing the delightful church as it does so. Adequate compensation is provided by the view of the church, standing in isolation beneath a backdrop of mature woodland. It may have existed in Saxon times, but the shapely castellated tower and knave are of fifteenth-century vintage. The unusual addition of a recent red pantile roof to the knave does not diminish its appeal.

Another treat is in store as the wooded confines of Brantingham Dale, the most popular valley within easy reach of Hull, are entered. The road continues through the valley bottom on a pleasing journey towards the crest of the Wolds, but the Way cleaves through avenues of spruce, elm and birch as it climbs the demanding valley side.

Rising from the dale, beyond the carpet of woodland, the path traverses the open Wolds countryside, which now comes into its own. Views become extensive and the village of South Cave can be discerned, huddling below cultivated slopes, some distance from the Way. The settlement's boundaries extend from the chalk Wolds to the floor of the clay vale, which is clothed with meadows and rich pasture. An ample ribbon of water, the Humber, can be seen winding through the plain, which stretches as far as the eye can see.

South Cave straddles the A1034 road that links Market Weighton and the bustling A63 road. It boasts a Gothic castle, built in 1804, which stands proudly behind the village. A decorative and imposing gateway guards the entrance to what is now the Cave Castle Hotel and Golf Complex. Although the castle's strategic

Harvest-time

importance has diminished, its turrets and battlements still provide an impressive façade for the modern hotel. An historic feel is engendered by four canons that protect its main entrance. The ornamental lake and attractive golf course add to the agreeable setting of this nineteenth-century landmark.

The next section of the Way takes a circuitous route to the strategic market town of Market Weighton, passing the twin settlements of North and South Newbald, as it does so. These lie in a sheltered hollow in the Wolds. Their cluster of cottages, many of rugged grey stone, or distinctively whitewashed, are a contrast to the striking North Newbald church, a monument to the local oolitic limestone, from which it is constructed. Some of the stone used to build the church, and also Beverley Minster, came from the nearby quarries, which originated in the thirteenth century. Dating back to Norman times, it is the most complete building of that period in the East Riding and its pale yellow walls still retain round-arched windows and medieval doorways.

Clear, open landscapes are displayed on Newbald Wold and its

Harvest-time

spaciousness is accentuated by the lack of habitation. However, on its western edge are several extensive beech plantations, which follow the contours and darken the skyline when viewed from the valley beneath. These mature arboreal bands were planted in the latter part of the eighteenth century.

At this point the Way runs parallel to the A1034 road, which follows the line of the former Roman road that linked York and Lincoln. In later times the great Methodist preacher, John Wesley, already eighty-five years old, was active in the area. Despite his great age, he set himself a punishing schedule. In one day he preached at nearby Sancton at nine o'clock in the morning, at Market Weighton at eleven, Pocklington at two, and York at six o'clock in the evening. To these four services could be added the two that he led on the previous day at Hull, a remarkable example of devotion and stamina that contributed to the establishment of many Methodist chapels in the area.

The Way crosses the A1079, Market Weighton to Beverley road, not far from the distinctive village of Kiplingcotes, best known for a famous annual event. The Kiplingcotes Derby is the oldest horse race in England, first run in 1519. Its route, covering a distance of approximately four miles, mainly comprises a rough track across fields and it ends on the verge of a metalled road. The race is open to horses of all ages and the prize money is meagre compared to the substantial funds involved in horse-racing today. The winner receives the princely sum of fifty pounds. Competition, however, is fierce and the race has been dominated in recent years by the nine times winner, veteran Ken Holmes, known locally as 'Galloping Grandad.' His winning streak came to an end this year when he was beaten into second place by a fifteen-year-old schoolgirl, Laura Crawford, who had to carry more than two stones of sand, in bags hung around her waist, to make up the required weight. Her proud father, who came third, revealed that he and Laura had been practising from 6am most mornings.

Since its inception, nearly 500 years ago, the race has taken place every year, even in the harsh winter of 1947. That particular year the organisers walked a horse round the course to ensure that it was safe to run.

Nearby Market Weighton stands to the west of the Roman road from Brough to Malton and has been a focal point of the East Riding for many centuries. It developed as a market town on the banks of the chalk stream that flows down from the Wolds and the settlement began to expand with the coming of the turnpike road from York, which passed through on its way to Beverley. The former turnpike is now the busy A1079, along which modern traffic speeds, bringing little respite to the town.

The Wolds Way pays its respects to Market Weighton by providing a detour to it, which veers west from the long-distance footpath as it approaches the nearby village of Goodmanham. Market Weighton offers a good range of accommodation to walkers, for it is one of the popular halting points on the Way. It is a place to rest and recuperate and savour the atmosphere of an East Riding market town that boasts buildings of character. Foremost amongst them are the three ancient inns, the Londesborough Arms, the Half Moon and the Old Bay Horse. The former is an imposing Georgian structure, whose impressive frontage and heraldic sign form a commanding façade that overlooks the main street.

A variety of shops line the main thoroughfare, beneath an irregular skyline of attractive roofs, which display a broad spectrum of age and colour. Behind these rows of multi-windowed buildings rises the conspicuous tower of All Saints Church, made more noticeable by its contrasting construction. The base is of conventional stone, but its upper section, a later addition, is of mature brick.

Market Weighton appears reluctant to reveal some of its best features. Tucked away behind the church is a tiny labyrinth of narrow streets and alleys that lead to a quiet square, known as The Green. This hideaway, with its tree-studded, grassy centre, is enhanced by quaint Georgian cottages and houses. Impressive doorways of that period add character to many of the buildings.

The railway, another contributor to Market Weighton's growth, came to the town by courtesy of the pioneer, George Hudson. He constructed a line from York in 1847, but nearly twenty years passed before it was extended to join the Hull to Bridlington link near Beverley.

The now forgotten and derelict station is a sad relic of a former grand edifice that boasted curvaceous stone-built bays, supported by impressive Tuscan columns.

Amongst the numerous memorials in the parish church of All Saints is one commemorating William Bradley, who lived in the town and grew to massive proportions. He was 7ft. 9ins tall, weighed twenty-seven stones and made his living in the bizarre world of fairground freaks. He travelled to fairs all around the country and died in 1820, at the age of only thirty-three.

The Way bypasses Goodmanham and heads for Londesborough, where it is re-joined by the alternative route that visits Market Weighton. It does so in the shadow of tumuli and barrows on the fringe of the Wolds that signify ancient occupation of this area.

An historic hamlet, Goodmanham has its origins in early pagan times. The Venerable Bede described it as 'this one-time place of idols,' a reference to the occasion when King Edwin and his high priest Coifi were converted from their heathen beliefs by the great missionary Paulinus. Their godless temple is believed to have occupied the site of the present church, which is mainly Norman.

Londesborough is even older, for its history goes back to Roman

Laura Crawford, winner of the 1999 Kiplingcotes Derby

times, as indicated by the discovery in 1895 of traces of the Roman road from Brough to Malton at the bottom of the lake in Londesborough Park. The Way follows a public bridleway through this sweeping parkland to the accompaniment of birdsong and the gaze of watchful deer.

The village may have been the site of a summer palace belonging to the Kings of Northumbria. In the fifteenth century it was known to be part of the vast estates belonging to the great Yorkshire dynasty, the Cliffords, thirteen of whom resided at Skipton Castle. Later, the land passed by marriage to the Earls of Burlington and then to the Cavendishes.

It was the third Earl of Burlington who laid out the vast park, with lakes, waterfalls and attractive terraces. He was a statesman and an architect and counted many writers and artists amongst his friends. Whilst on a Grand Tour of Italy, in 1715, he became a disciple of Palladio, the renowned Italian architect. On his return he promoted an English edition of his idol's work.

Kiplingcotes Derby sign

He was also a friend of David Garrick, and he planted a splendid avenue of elms in the park, in memory of the accomplished actor. During some of his visits, the local vicar frequently sought advice from the great thespian on reading the scriptures in church.

Londesborough Hall was unfortunately demolished by one of the Cavendish family, the sixth Duke of Devonshire, in 1819. So distraught was he when he revisited the scene of his destruction that he shed tears of remorse for his rash deed. The blow was undoubtedly softened by the sale of the estate in 1845 for nearly a half a million pounds.

The purchaser was George Hudson, who was engaged in planning the line from York to Market Weighton, and he routed it so that it passed the estate. Here, he built his own private station, near the village of Shiptonthorpe, and created an impressive tree-lined drive, two miles long, which linked it to his house. Hudson's stay in the area was short, for his financial empire collapsed in 1849 and he was forced to sell the estate. The avenue that he created can still be seen from the roadside near Londesborough, but unfortunately, the station no longer exists.

On the Wold above Londesborough lies Burnby Chalk Pit, a vast quarry, which has yielded huge quantities of material and provided work for men of the locality. Farming, however, has been the mainstay of the Wolds for centuries, but in the 1930's it was in depression.

Farms were becoming derelict, or being worked by their owners for lack of tenants. Long rows of wagon sheds stood almost empty. The Wolds wagon, peculiar to the district, was about to be superceded by the tractor and the combined harvester. In its day it was an impressive vehicle, pulled by horses or oxen, with overhanging sides to hold the corn. A wagoner had one of the most responsible jobs on a farm and normally deputised for the foreman, or hind, as he was sometimes known. He was often the proud possessor of a whip, with as many brass rings as he could afford on it.

When the corn harvest began, the Wolds was a scene of intense activity. First came the reapers, who cut the corn with great skill. They were followed by men who gathered it into 'stooks,' (bundles). In some fields the bundles were left to dry, in others they were loaded onto the Wolds wagons, which rumbled along the narrow lanes to where great stacks were being built near the farmhouses.

During the depression, farmers needed money so badly that they threshed as soon as possible following the harvest. Many did not bother to use the discarded stems for thatching the stacks. In the once tidy fields and farmyards, straw was left lying around for weeks, for want of labour to clear it.

Farm hands were often taken on at 'Hirings,' as they were known, which were also used as meeting places for families and friends, particularly at Martinmas, when a holiday was celebrated. There was often great merriment at these affairs, but sometimes it boiled over into ugly scenes. Parties were common, with plenty to eat and drink. The occasional toffee supper was held, where toffee was made round a fire and rolled and eaten whilst still warm.

At the Hirings, farmers would sometimes pick out men and lads, merely because they liked the looks of them, but more often because they knew something about their worth. One farmer was heard to declare: 'I allus pick a lad wi' a cap. He'll be a good worker, will a lad wi' a cap.'

The next significant town in the vicinity of the Wolds Way is Pocklington, on whose outskirts lie the renowned Burnby Hall Gardens, which contain one of the finest collections of water-lilies in Europe. The creator of these splendid gardens was Major Percy Marlborough Stewart, who devoted thirty years of hard work to them. He was a pioneer of travel during the early days of motoring and in the early nineteen-hundreds he and his wife encircled the globe in their car. In 1926 he ceased his world travel and settled at Burnby Hall, where he developed the gardens and maintained the estate. Lakes were created, brimming with fish and in 1935 he planted water-lilies in them. There are now innumerable varieties, presenting colourful kaleidoscopes, which blend amiably with the rich diversity of plants in the surrounding gardens. The local authority bought the property following Major Stewart's death in 1962 and converted the hall into its administration centre. At the bequest of the major, the gardens and the Stewart Collection were donated to the people of Pocklington.

Crossing the B1246 road near Pocklington, the Way heads for Millington, a village that squats in a quiet, fertile valley, surrounded at one time by pastures that were renowned throughout the Wolds. In former times the main field of over 400 acres was used as common pasture, shared by all the farmers in the district. Each farmer rented a number of 'gaits,' which represented pasturage for six sheep, or four sheep with their lambs. Until recently Millington Pastures denoted the survival of the old way of sheep-farming in the Wolds, but in the 1960's they were enclosed and sown with crops.

The approach to Millington is impressive. The Way passes above the village along Millington Heights, a bridleway that follows the line of a Roman road. It presents a glorious high-level traverse, offering long-distance views across the expansive Vale of York. Millington appears a village in miniature, nestling beneath cultivated slopes; its cluster of red roofs an oasis of colour in a pastoral landscape.

A path leaves the Way to descend the valley and cross tree-lined Millington Beck, which glides through its floor, before entering the appealing village. Its focal point, by the tiny green, is a boon to

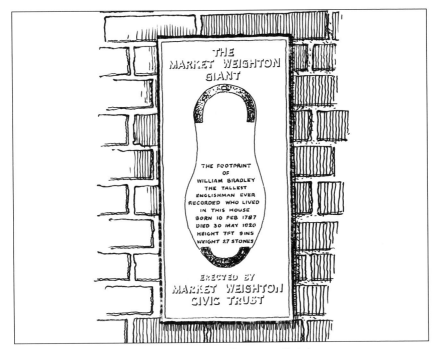

Sign on the wall of William Bradley's house

walkers. The inviting sign, 'The Ramblers Rest Tearooms,' gladdens the heart of weary Wolds Way trampers, with its promise of rest and refreshment. On fine spring days, groups of walkers and cyclists can be seen reclining on the green, beneath bowers of flowering cherry.

One warm and sunny afternoon, my companion and I were relaxing outside the tearooms when the tranquility was shattered by the roar of engines. Our eyes widened as a stream of ancient motor-cycles appeared and their riders dismounted. The venerable machines were most impressive. Frameworks shone and gleaming chrome dazzled in the sunlight. I recognised some of the models, which made me feel my age.

One of the riders, who obviously lavished loving care on his mount, explained that he was a member of a vintage motor-cycle club that was taking part in a local rally. He pointed out some of the oldest machines that were built in the 1920's, but looked as good as new. As he was doing this, members of the club, who were not adept at route-finding, straggled into view.

The Wolds Inn, Huggate

The Way progresses to Huggate, a quiet village that stands at the junction of several minor Wolds roads. It must have been an important halt at one time, for the place possesses an ancient hostelry, the Wolds Inn, which occupies a prominent roadside position. This brightly-painted and homely inn is enhanced by a large, eye-catching sign, which hangs above its entrance. The painting upon it, a faithful reproduction of the hostelry, is quite stunning. Two dumpy stone pillars signify the gateway to the adjacent car park. They are also vividly-painted and display the names 'Huggate' and 'Wolds Inn' respectively.

The village appears as silent and deserted as the Wolds landscape that surrounds it, but it does possess a certain charm. Tree-lined gardens flank the main street and old properties mingle with the new. In a secluded corner hides the dainty church with a slender spire that overlooks the nearby Old School House, a charming rustic cottage.

Not far from the village lies another of the numerous gashes in the landscape from which chalk is hewn. Thankfully the quarry is not visible from the road but motorists will be well aware of its presence. All the surrounding lanes are liberally coated with white dust, deposited by the heavy lorries that carry away vast tons of crushed chalk.

It is a short journey from Huggate to Fridaythorpe, which straddles the busy A166, York to Great Driffield road. Unlike many of the other villages that lie on, or near to, the Wolds Way, this is an upland settlement. The most attractive part of Fridaythorpe is out of sight of the main road and the church is demurely hidden behind a farm. In keeping with Huggate, the village has an old, strategically placed, inn, offering hospitality to passing walkers and motorists. It stands within sight of a small, but engaging pond, frequented by the local army of ducks that alternately swim in its glistening water or bask on its grassy surrounds.

On Ordnance Survey maps of the area the names of some of the large, open fields can be seen. One such field occupied much of the land surrounding Fridaythorpe and to the north and east lay similar expanses, namely, Towthorpe Field and South Field.

The A166 road provides a convenient artery for exploring the network of quiet lanes that penetrate the central Wolds. These peaceful thoroughfares offer splendid vantage-points from which to view the dry, grassy valleys that wind between the Wolds. In early summer these uncultivated emerald channels are at their finest, bedecked with flowering gorse and topped with brilliant-white hawthorne blossom.

Several of these lanes can be followed to Thixendale, one of the gems of the Wolds Way that lies in a deep cleft in the hills. The southern approach to the village is down a steep, winding hill, from which, a commanding aerial view of this cloistered outpost is presented. Neat rows of buildings flank its main street, which comes to an abrupt end beneath a glaring band of white, a track known as the 'chalk road' that snakes over a distant hill. The light greens of the valley floor give way to darker pastures that clothe the steep surrounding slopes, which are liberally studded with bushes and fringed with delicate bands of trees. On top of the surrounding Wolds, a dark green carpet of crops intermingles with bands of furrowed soil.

In the village itself, opposite the church, stands the village store, with its adjacent café. This pleasant halt, unfortunately hidden behind the store, offers a friendly welcome. It is a veritable oasis for walkers and is very popular with cyclists.

Despite its seemingly remote location, Thixendale has six minor roads leading to it and it also forms the hub of a network of sixteen dry valleys. In former times its water supply came from nearby springs, whose issues were collected in a concrete tank and piped to several taps in the main street. The surplus from the tank continued as a chalk stream through the village.

The northern Wolds are entered beyond Thixendale and the locality contains several deserted villages. The most famous of all, Wharram Percy, lies at the end of our journey. This long-abandoned site has been an interesting milestone in the archaeology of medieval England. The Church of St. Martin is the only surviving feature of the original village. It stands in a lonely setting near the Wolds Way, the gaunt remains of its tower forming a landmark in a secluded, fertile valley. Most of the building is ruinous. The knave roof has gone and its hollow windows afford no protection against the unforgiving winds that scour the vale.

The church formerly served not only Wharram Percy, but also the nearby villages of Thixendale, Burdale, Raisthorpe and Towthorpe. All but Thixendale are now abandoned and the ruined church, together with its surrounds, is owned by English Heritage.

Since 1950 the site has been subjected to archaeological study. The original village was identified by aerial photography and numerous excavations have revealed the outlines of medieval houses, cottages and paddocks. Many important finds have been revealed, but much of the excavations have been filled in to avoid danger to cattle that graze the valley.

The early settlement of Wharram Percy was situated on a hill above the church. In the late twelfth century the Percy family built a large manor house nearby. Eventually the village was extended and another manor house was built on a different site.

Around 1350, Wharram Percy was ravaged by the Black Death, but the village was not completely emptied by this scourge. It survived and the Hilton family took over the estate in the fifteenth century and did considerable rebuilding.

Recent discoveries of pottery confirm that habitation continued until 1500, when the cloth making industry was taking hold. Wool was in great demand, making it more profitable for landowners to

The Waggoners' Monument at Sledmere

rear sheep, instead of growing corn. The village lost the livelihood of its menfolk, for ploughmen and agricultural workers were no longer required. The parish became an extensive sheep-run and the people drifted away to find work. Houses collapsed and grass gradually grew over the remains of the village.

In addition to the ruined church, a row of cottages and a small pond occupy what is now a tranquil site, which once reverberated with the sounds of a lively community. Since Saxon times successive dams have been constructed across the valley to gather water from hillside springs and the most recent of them created the current pond that would formerly have been stocked with fish and used to provide power for a mill.

On the end wall of the cottages is mounted a large sign bearing the name 'Wharram.' It formerly adorned Wharram station that adjoined the site. First erected in 1901, it was removed in 1940, due to the threat of a German invasion, and discarded. In1967 it was rescued from obscurity, eventually refurbished and erected in its present position by the excavators of Wharram Percy in 1975.

The station stood on the old Malton to Great Driffield railway line that ran through the valley and onwards to Burdale. Its route to Burdale followed a striking deep-sided valley, known locally as Fimber Bottom. Today only a quiet road threads through the scenic cleft, but it provides a stimulating drive that passes a glittering pond set deep within it.

The line was opened in 1863. It was a tribute to engineering expertise, because it had to negotiate steep gradients and the mile-long Burdale tunnel. The Wolds farmers relied heavily upon it and cargoes of chalk from the quarries at Burdale and Wharram were transported. The passenger service was discontinued in 1950 and goods were only carried for another eight years.

No account of a journey through the Wolds would be complete without a mention of Sledmere House that stands a few miles from Wharram Percy. In 1787, the mansion was converted to its present style by Wyatt, a renowned architect. Two wings were added to its Queen Anne style predecessor and the complete structure was faced with Nottinghamshire stone. It stands in an elevated position amidst a vast sweep of parkland that was laid out in semi-formal design by Capability Brown. Within the park are formal gardens, extensive lawns, a lake and an Italian style fountain. So expansive is the park that when it was created, every house in the old Sledmere village had to be demolished. However, by the time that alterations to the house were complete, a new village had been built around the northern fringe of the park.

The house and grounds are open to the public and they form a tribute to the pioneering owners, the Sykes family, whose efforts helped to shape the Wolds into their present form. Their story begins in Leeds during the sixteenth century when William Sykes made his fortune in wool. His grandson, Richard, purchased the Manor of Leeds from the Crown in the seventeenth century and his fortunes prospered to such an extent that he was able to hand over huge estates to his four sons. A later Richard Sykes inherited the Tudor house at Sledmere in 1748. He demolished it and replaced it with the Queen Anne style building.

When Richard died in 1761 he was succeeded by his brother the Reverend Mark Sykes, who became the only clergyman to be made a baronet. This honour arose largely at the request of his son, Christopher, who had been offered it by William Pitt, in recognition of his pioneering agricultural work on the estates.

Christopher succeeded to the title and the estates when Sir Mark died in 1783 and it was he who directed Wyatt in the conversion of Sledmere House. Taking up the whole of the first floor for a great library, he laid the foundations for a splendid collection of rare books, many of which he had collected during his grand tour of 1770.

His contribution to the shaping of the Wolds began when he married Elizabeth Tatton, joint heir to the Egerton Estates, and used some of her fortune to begin his pioneering work in agriculture. He enclosed vast sheep-walks on the Wolds around Sledmere and began large-scale ploughing and cultivation. Over 50,000 larches were planted to provide shelter and he erected many farms, complete with barns and stables. The surrounding road network was also improved, many miles of new thoroughfare being added. Sir Christopher insisted that these had wide grass verges so that poor people could graze their stock on them.

When he died in 1801, owner of vast tracts of the Wolds, a domed memorial was erected in his memory. It stands by the roadside in Sledmere, opposite the main entrance to the house. To his eternal credit, Sir Christopher had developed what was once a blank swathe of countryside into one of the most productive and prosperous agricultural areas in Britain.

The fourth baronet, Sir Tatton Sykes, who became a legendary figure throughout Yorkshire, was a great character. He inherited the

Sledmere Stud from his brother and continued to increase it until it became the largest in England. A man of immense energy and determination, he once rode the sixty-three miles from Sledmere to Pontefract to take part in a race that afternoon. He then went to Doncaster and, after an overnight stop, rode to Lincoln for another race. On two occasions he rode to Aberdeen to compete in Scotland's greatest race, the Welter Stakes. As soon as those races were over he galloped back to Doncaster each time in order to watch his own horses competing in the St. Leger. He was also a frequent visitor to London, which involved a four-day journey from Sledmere.

His son, the second Sir Tatton, was a social pioneer and philanthropist. He spent one and a quarter million pounds on the building and restoration of Wolds churches, in addition to providing and maintaining several schools.

In 1911 the house was gutted by fire, which destroyed much of its interior, but thankfully the movable contents, including furniture by Chippendale and Sheraton, were saved. Another stroke of good fortune was the preservation of the original drawings for the plasterwork that were compiled by Joseph Rhodes, who had worked with the Adam brothers. These graphics were used in the re-creation of the interior décor, which was returned to its original state by the architect W.H.Brierly

To complete the story of Sledmere House, Sir Richard Sykes, the seventh baronet, opened it to the public in 1965. To his delight he found that visitors treated it with great respect, particularly as it has been the home of an outstanding family that has survived many turbulent generations of English history.

Their memorial lies all around as you travel through the surrounding Wolds, but probably the most spectacular of all is a slender tower, 120 feet high, that was erected in 1865 in commemoration of the fourth baronet, the second Sir Tatton. This impressive obelisk has panels in relief at its base that show him surveying his extensive estates.

Richard Whiteley

CHAPTER THREE

Countdown to Success

Richard Whiteley firmly believes that life is littered with instances of 'if only.' How many of us, looking back on our lives, say to ourselves, 'If only I had done this or, if only that had happened?' In Richard's case it did happen, because it was thanks to several twists of fate that he joined the infant Yorkshire Television at the time when a local news programme entitled *Calendar* was about to be launched. From then onwards he has counted himself very fortunate to be handed such a golden opportunity.

Not only was it an opportune career move but it allowed him to return to his native county, for which he has an enduring affection. He was born in the Duke of York Nursing Home in Bradford, but was soon moved to his home in Ferncliffe Drive, Baildon. The year was 1943 and the pleasant hill-top section of the village was much smaller and more rural than it is today.

Richard's initial memories are of a happy early childhood, which was enhanced by his gratifying surroundings. The view over the wall of his parents' back garden comprised fields and meadows stretching as far as the eye can see. A great source of happiness was the closest of those fields, which was a working cornfield. Each autumn, at harvest-time, Richard could be found there, riding with the very affable farmer on the small Fordson tractor that pulled an old-fashioned threshing machine, or playing in the stooks of fresh-cut corn, which provided natural dens. Fifty years on, he still vividly remembers the smell of the oily tractor and the unmistakable aroma of the harvest.

Ferncliffe Drive leads to one of Baildon's natural attributes, a conspicuous landmark that lies within the shadow of Baildon Moor. Craggy Baildon Bank provides an excellent adventure playground that lay on his very doorstep. He played a variety of games around its prominent rocks and on the grassy lower slopes that tumble down to Baildon Green. The sinister, but exciting quarry, hewn into its side, was another great attraction. A favourite pastime was throwing stones from its rim into its enticing depths and counting the number of

Baildon in quieter times

seconds it took them to reach the bottom. An additional benefit of this gash in the hillside was its suitability for furtive smoking.

Their neighbours in Ferncliffe Drive, the Whittakers, were staunch Methodists and Arthur Whittaker, who was second master at Salts School, introduced him to the Wesleyan chapel, where he attended Sunday morning service and Sunday School. He also joined the Methodist cub pack, but never graduated to the scouts because he eventually went to Heather Bank Preparatory School in Bingley and did not normally arrive home before 6.30 pm.

In 1953 his parents moved to another house that was barely a stone's throw away, in neighbouring Greencliffe Avenue. Whilst living there, Richard began helping a local newsagent, known only as Stubbs, with his newspaper round. This proved to be a very enjoyable enterprise, particularly when delivering to the houses in Greencliffe Avenue. There was one imposing detatched house that always held his attention, principally because of the pond in its

The house with the pond – Greencliffe Avenue, Baildon

front garden. He thought it amazing that the doctor who lived there at the time should have a pond in his garden. The property was built by the parents of Ronnie Burnet, who became captain of Yorkshire County Cricket Club. Richard, who had already developed an interest in cricket, despite his own lack of proficiency in the sport, knew of Ronnie Burnet through his captaincy of Baildon during the 1950's, when they were one of the leading clubs in the Bradford League.

Richard has many other pleasant recollections of his childhood in Baildon. He loved the village centre with its homely atmosphere and sense of community. This is a trait that has remained throughout his life, an enjoyment of small, tight-knit communities that foster a sense of belonging. The ancient stocks, the Potted Meat Stick and his rides on the heavily laden single-decker buses that strained up Baildon Hill, all contributed to the pleasing fabric of life in the village.

In the pre-computer age of the early 1950's, his family's home entertainment consisted of a radiogram, which housed a radio and an automatic turntable suitable for playing 78 rpm and EP records. In addition to providing enjoyment, it also constituted an impressive item of furniture.

Weekly helpings of *Take it From Here* and *The Billy Cotton Band Show* were dispensed by the radio and the family's limited record collection contained the *Donkey Serenade,* a tune which remains firmly lodged in Richard's memory. He recalls that the first record he ever purchased had *Rudolph the Red-Nosed Reindeer* on one side and *Teddy Bears' Picnic* on the other.

The exciting new medium of television was beginning to take hold in 1952 and Richard began to pester his parents to purchase a set. One day he could hardly contain himself when a van turned up at the gate from Jefferson's, the local radio and television suppliers, situated on the corner of Westgate and Towngate. A shiny new television set, with a 12inch screen, was delivered to the house. It became a pride and joy and augured well for viewing the forthcoming coronation of Queen Elizabeth II.

Watching television in those early days aroused Richard's enthusiasm for the medium, just as youngsters today find computers exciting. All programmes were transmitted live and output was restricted to evenings only. As the first programme did not commence until 8pm, he considered it a special treat to stay up on a Sunday evening to watch *What's My Line.*

It was television's hardware that really attracted him and he watched keenly for mistakes, such as cameras straying within shot. He was determined to become involved in this exciting new technology, ideally as a cameraman.

One Saturday lunchtime, he was returning from school in Bingley, where attendance was required on Saturday mornings, when he spotted a large van parked on the road that crosses Baildon Moor. It had green livery emblazoned with 'BBC Television Service' in gold lettering and the coat of arms bearing the words 'Nation Shall Speak Peace Unto Nation.'

Richard now understands that it was merely a 'link' van, the most unglamorous part of a film unit, which relays the signal to a transmitter. At the time, despite it containing no cameras or associated equipment, he found it unbelievable that such a vehicle should park a short distance from his home. He wanted to scrutinise the van but the BBC engineers were evasive, which only

Giggleswick School

View over Giggleswick and Settle

Baildon Bank

Kirkby Malham

increased his determination to learn more about, and eventually work in, television.

Heather Bank School occupied a large house adjacent to Lady Lane and the Prince of Wales Park in Bingley. Inaugurated after the Second World War by Colin Griffiths and his wife, Ida, it was run on strict disciplinary lines. Most of the forty-five boys who attended travelled by trolley-bus from Bradford and walked up Park Road to the school.

This provided the degree of exercise that was considered necessary, but the Baildon boys, who normally came by car, were required to alight above the Prince of Wales Park and walk the rest of the distance. If they obeyed this instruction they were only required to run round the school garden once, but if they were dropped off at the school gates, they had to run round the garden twice.

Each lunchtime the boys were interrogated as to where they had alighted and the number of times that they had run round the garden. Truthful answers were normally forthcoming, despite the fact that that the tutors had no means of checking the boys' replies.

It was expected that all pupils would be in bed at a reasonable hour and they were also questioned at lunchtime concerning the time that they had retired on the previous evening. Richard's friend, Peter Colman, also from Baildon, was continually in trouble for staying up late and watching television.

Despite the strict discipline, Richard was very happy at the school and did well academically, eventually becoming a prefect. Because of his limited sporting ability, Richard was never selected for any of the school teams. He did, however, play the subsidiary roles of linesman for the football team and scorer for the cricket team, so he was able to sample a taste of first team life.

At the age of thirteen Richard moved to Giggleswick School, near Settle, as a boarder. Being quite bright he went straight into the fourth form amongst fourteen and fifteen year-olds, thereby missing out the first year. Consequently he took his 'O' level exams at the age of fourteen and his 'A' levels two years later.

Unfortunately his late start meant his missing a basic grounding in science, but he was proficient at English, his best subject. Richard counts himself lucky to have been taught by two outstanding English masters, the first being John Dean, who was

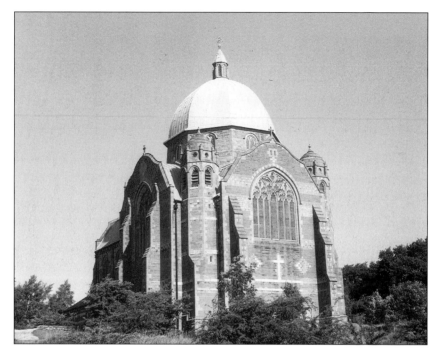

Giggleswick School Chapel

also his housemaster. Distinguished through his membership of the MCC, he came from a respected family and his father was the Colonial Governor, Sir Arthur Dean. One of the 'old school' of teaching, he was meticulous and thorough, acquiring a reputation for extreme tidiness because of his habit of picking up litter from the school premises.

The second of Richard's revered tutors was Russell Harty, who some years later became a familiar face on television. A younger generation of teacher, he brought a breath of fresh air to the school, through his liveliness and inspirational qualities. Modern in outlook, he had a wide circle of friends and acquaintances. Amongst these was a particular friend who often visited the school; a young Oxford don by the name of Alan Bennett.

Sport was a compulsory part of the school curriculum and Richard tried hard to contribute. He smilingly recalls the period when he played rugby three times a week for twelve weeks without laying a hand on the ball. This, he declares, is a record that is unlikely to be broken. He could not run quickly enough to get the

Richard's boyhood heroes – Yorkshire CCC (1951)
Left to right – Hutton, Trueman, Leadbeater, Wilson, Brennan,
Yardley, Appleyard, Watson, Wardle, Lester, Halliday

ball and it was never passed to him. The master in charge of these games took pity on him. Russell Harty, who hated refereeing as much as Richard hated playing, would instruct him to return the ball to the changing rooms after the final whistle, so that he could at least hold it in his hands.

As further proof of his lack of rugby prowess, his mother maintained that his shorts never needed washing and were still in pristine condition after the twelve weeks in question.

Giggleswick School stands in an ideal position for outdoor pursuits, surrounded by limestone fells, perfect for cross-country runs. Richard remembers the many occasions that the boys were required to climb Attermire Scar before breakfast. He also recalls finding a suitable hiding place, at the outset of cross-country runs, in which he would skulk until the other boys returned from their exertions, whereupon he would return with them to the finish.

Regular P.E. sessions were also held, in all weathers and Richard did not relish these. He frequently found himself doing punishment drill, which consisted of a further fifteen minutes of the dreaded exercise.

Once again Richard was on the sidelines as far as cricket was concerned but he grew to love the picturesque setting of the school ground, and the splendid chapel that overlooks it. From the vantage-point provided by this excellent cricket ground, on which any county side would be pleased to play, he could look over Giggleswick and Settle to a dramatic backdrop of limestone hills. He has grown to love limestone, but did not appreciate its attributes at that time. Now, when he frequently re-visits he is lost in admiration for the area.

His appetite is whetted before he reaches Settle, for as he rounds a bend on the approaching A65 road an unforgettable panorama unfolds. The elevated school chapel with its unique dome can be clearly seen and beyond, impressive Giggleswick Scar rises amidst a green landscape slashed with silver. The majestic hump of distant Ingleborough completes a scene that he finds intensely moving.

Richard is genuinely envious of the present pupils of Giggleswick School, who, he believes, enjoy much more favourable conditions. He would love to share their privilege of opening the dormitory curtains each morning to expose the inspiring view, over the neat stone buildings and distinctive church of Giggleswick, to the rugged profile of limestone fells across the valley.

The setting of the school has nurtured Richard's abiding love for the Dales and he once considered setting up home in the Craven, or Ribblesdale areas. Another vale that appeals to him is Wensleydale, a particular favourite because of its spaciousness and wide vistas.

When time permits Richard enjoys driving through the Dales and there are two scenic routes that he finds singularly rewarding. The first is the road from Settle to Kirkby Malham, which offers a feast of extensive views, particularly on fine days when resplendent bracken and heather bask beneath clear blue skies. Second is the journey through upper Wharfedale and Langstrothdale that leads over the bleak, but evocative, watershed of Fleet Moss to the popular market town of Hawes in Wensleydale.

It was thanks to the excellent tuition of John Dean and Russell Harty that Richard achieved a place at Cambridge University, where he read English. Unfortunately he felt a little out of his depth, but he was determined to pursue his goal of joining the BBC. The problem was that many other students had the same objective and there was a great demand for places. His chances of success seemed slight, so he explored other avenues of entry. He tried acting and directing as another possibility, believing that he might be accepted as a thespian.

Whilst at Giggleswick Richard had gained a little theatrical experience by assisting Russell Harty with a production of *The Merchant of Venice* and for his endeavours he was given the elevated title of Assistant Producer. During his first term at Cambridge Richard directed *Roots*, but he eventually realised that he was not cut out for theatrical pursuits.

He changed direction once more and joined the University newspaper, *Varsity,* which circulated a weekly edition each Friday. The paper was very professionally produced in the organisation's own premises and it operated at a substantial profit, gleaned through advertising. In his third year Richard became Editor and despite the time-consuming nature of such a position, he found it fairly easy to combine the work with his studies.

This substantial sideline probably contributed towards the third-class degree that Richard obtained at the end of his course, but his *Varsity* experience was soon to open many doors for him. When he left university he did not apply to the BBC, mainly because the appointments board that he attended encouraged him not to, in the light of the heavy demand for places.

By chance, whilst Editor of the paper, he was asked to go to Norwich to be interviewed on *About Anglia*, that particular television network's equivalent of *Calendar*. His interviewer was Michael Partington, who asked him to outline the work involved in the circulation of what was probably the most comprehensive and substantial student's newspaper in existence at that time. Richard duly related the tasks entailed in producing the sixty-four-page edition, complete with colour supplement.

After the interview Michael divulged that he too was a Yorkshireman, who hailed from Harrogate. He also revealed that he was a former editor of the *Pudsey News* and he asked Richard what he wanted to do when he left university. Richard replied that he

Richard with Carol Vorderman on Countdown

wished to work in television but would not make it into the BBC. Michael informed him that ITN recruited two trainees each year, which resulted in Richard's application for a position with that company.

He was granted an interview, as a result of which, he was offered one of the two traineeships. During his three years with ITN he had a backroom role, which included scriptwriting.

In March 1968 Richard left ITN to join the fledgling Yorkshire Television and one of the first people that he met was Michael Partington, who had joined the previous month. People of varying backgrounds were in the process of being recruited from all parts of the country and the time was ripe for new talent and innovation. Donald Baverstock, the entrepreneurial Programme Controller, had just masterminded a local news programme entitled *Calendar,* onto which Richard was recruited. Donald had earlier devised the highly successful *Tonight* whilst working for the BBC. Everything pioneered on that programme was incorporated into *Calendar,* such as the magazine slot, film report, down-the-line interview and the controversial one plus

Langstrothdale

two studio debate. All these components were supplied with well-delivered, humorous scripts.

The programme was destined to become a resounding success and Richard believes that its strong title has contributed to its continuing appeal over the thirty-one years of its existence. It was begun with an untried team and Richard had no visions of appearing on-screen, a task for which he had no experience. They were all in the deep end together and Richard was surprisingly instructed to read the news, which he duly did without disaster. The format eventually settled down, with Richard and Austin Mitchell as co-presenters, until Austin left in 1977, to become an MP.

Richard remained with *Calendar* for twenty-seven happy years and his only reason for leaving was the increasing demands of *Countdown*. The programme became engraved on his heart, for he was involved with it for a large proportion of his working life. He experienced the joy of living in Yorkshire and working for two inspirational leaders. The first was the previously mentioned Donald Baverstock, who was succeeded by Paul Fox, the last of the television dinosaurs. Paul was a powerful man, in every respect, powerful both in Yorkshire and in ITV.

During his years with *Calendar,* Richard felt that Yorkshire was an admirable place to be. He still does, of course and much prefers the quality of life in his home county to moving south. There is no desire on his part to gravitate to London, as many successful people are apt to do.

The programme that has brought him national recognition is *Countdown,* which began as a local presentation in the summer of 1982. It was one of several spin-offs from *Calendar* and initially was broadcast on Monday evenings only. Originally entitled *Calendar Countdown,* its potential was immediately detected by Richard through its impact upon the public and the staff at Yorkshire Television. Following its initial popularity it was vetted by the infant Channel 4, who decided to run it four days per week in the late afternoon. The channel was so new that it had not begun transmission at that time. When it did, on November 2nd at 4-45pm, *Countdown* was the first programme to be shown. Richard is immensely proud of the fact that as its presenter, his face was the first to be seen on Channel 4. The initial contract was for four weeks only, but the programme is still going strong after seventeen years.

In addition to his work on *Calendar* and *Countdown,* Richard was involved with a variety of other satisfying projects. Amongst these was *Calendar People,* a chat show that was filmed before a live audience in the mid-1970's. Richard remembers the show with particular affection because many of its participants are now deceased and he believes that it represents an enduring social document. James Herriot, Joe Kagan, Albert Modley, Harry Corbett and Wilfred Pickles were amongst the notable guests. One of its highlights was the episode that featured Len Hutton, the Yorkshire and England cricketer. The complete Yorkshire cricket team of the 1950's, whose members were his boyhood heroes, was in the audience on that inspiring occasion. Richard was very proud that the very successful group of players, who were all of England calibre, had participated in the programme.

Many other well known personalities appeared on the show, including the Earl and Countess of Harewood and Harvey Smith and in total there were roughly twenty episodes of that popular mirror on Yorkshire life.

View over Wensleydale

Baildon Methodist Chapel

Another programme that Richard found very satisfying was the *Richard Whiteley Show,* which was transmitted during the 1990's. It was an enjoyable piece of fun in the form of a variety show that was intended to enliven Sunday evenings. The programme also indulged his appetite for live, spontaneous shows. In fact he has always preferred studio work to outside locations.

Into his busy schedule, covering a period of thirty years, have been slotted a variety of political interviews. As a result of these encounters Richard has kept abreast of major political activity and become friendly with many MP's.

Richard's varied and comprehensive output over the years has earned another accolade. Sir David Frost refers to him as the person who has appeared more times on television than anyone, because of his *Calendar* and *Countdown* successes. Richard modestly responds to the compliment by saying he is forever grateful that a major television company grew up only a few miles from his home.

An additional, more light-hearted accolade is his enrolment as the unofficial mayor of Wetwang, an attractive village in the Yorkshire Wolds. Unfortunately this community of around 300

Bolton Castle, Wensleydale

residents does not qualify for such an office, but Richard regards his appointment as a bit of fun that has aroused considerable publicity and helped to put the village on the map. It all began when he mentioned Wetwang on *Countdown*, as a place with an interesting and humorous name. He announced on the programme that he would be honoured to become its mayor and thought no more about it until he received a letter from the PTA of the village school, inviting him to accept the office. He made several visits to Wetwang and appeared on television dressed in his mayoral attire, which helped to promote the jocular interlude.

He also recalls mentioning Wig Wig, in Shropshire, on the programme, adding that he would like to become mayor of that village, because he would then be a 'big-wig in Wig Wig.'

Richard's sense of humour has played a large part in endearing him to the public, but a keen intellect and sensitivity remain hidden behind his light-hearted façade. The latter quality is aptly demonstrated by the depth of feeling that he holds for his roots and in particular for the traditions and community spirit of Giggleswick School.

One of his abiding memories is the aura of the school chapel. He admires its wonderful architecture and he believes that no pupil can avoid being affected by what takes place there. Inspiring music, massed voices and a feeling of closeness to God form its most memorable attributes. Richard recalls the end of term services as very moving occasions, held in darkness, apart from two candles, in memory of the Second World War blackout. The splendid finale was an organ rendition of *Nimrod,* during which, even burly rugger captains were known to shed a tear.

It is not surprising that Richard's choice of site for a memorial seat, dedicated to his father, is outside the door of the chapel. The inscription on the seat is as follows:

In Grateful Memory
T.K. Whiteley O. G. 1926-29
Placed Here by Richard Whiteley
President O. G. Club 1993-94

His father was a pupil during the period outlined in the inscription and one of the significant recollections of his time at Giggleswick School is the day in 1927 when all the boys climbed the hill to the chapel in order to watch the eclipse.

CHAPTER FOUR

The Enduring Dale

Tucked away beyond Kilnsey Crag lies Littondale, a peaceful offshoot valley of Wharfedale. It possesses a timeless air, seemingly untouched by the ruthless hand of time. The narrow ribbon of road that snakes through the dale is confronted at its head by the barrier of Horsehead Moor. Realising that the challenge of those moorland heights is too great it swiftly changes course, taking the easier option of a journey, through adjoining Silverdale, to Ribblesdale.

Undiscerning people assume that Littondale comes to an abrupt end and is therefore not a convenient through route to other parts of the Dales. They do not know what they are missing. A drive along its enticing reaches and through its attractive villages offers great rewards, not least the vistas of its limestone scars and bracken-coated fell sides, ribbed in parts with ancient cultivation terraces. It is a splendid foil to the adjacent, better-known valleys of Wharfedale and Ribblesdale. Many time worn tracks cross its higher reaches, formally trodden by monks, Bronze Age traders and packmen. The remains of lead-mine workings and an Iron Age Settlement can be discovered on the crests of its enfolding hills.

Pass under the shadow of the distinctive overhang on Kilnsey Crag's rugged profile, formed by a retreating glacier, and you will soon reach the inviting entrance to Littondale. Here the sparkling River Skirfare greets the Wharfe amidst a tapestry of green meadows, interlaced with limestone walls and adorned by a sprinkling of barns, so characteristic of the Yorkshire Dales landscape.

A choice of two roads up the initial part of the dale is available. These thoroughfares travel, on opposite sides of the Skirfare, to Arncliffe, the most familiar settlement of the valley. The wider of the two leaves the B6160, Kettlewell road, just before Skirfare Bridge is reached. If the minor road is chosen, access is gained by means of a cattle grid, immediately beyond the aforementioned bridge. This narrow byroad should be accessed with care, for it is

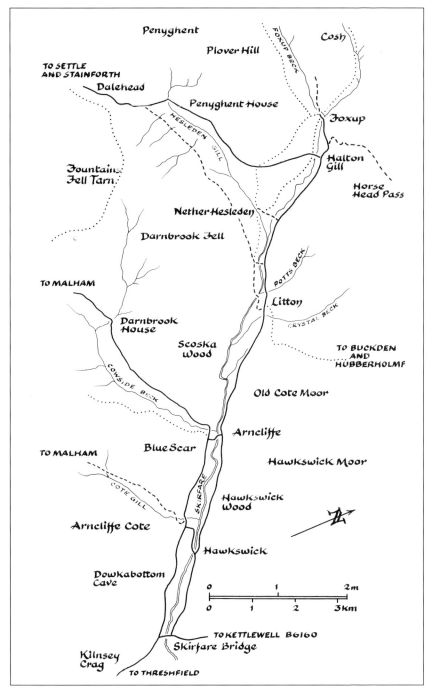

Littondale

single track with very few passing places.

Alternatively, cars may be parked on the extensive field that borders this minor road, as it begins its journey beneath the shadow of Firth Fell. There is a moderate fee for the privilege of leaving vehicles on the farmer's meadow, and the energetic may wish to explore the sculptured limestone crags of Firth Fell that beckon from the heights.

Above the crags, sepia tinted moorland rises to a crest, pock-marked by bell pits and shake holes, remnants of former lead-mining activity. Evidence can also be found on these heights of ancient enclosures and settlements.

During autumn and winter the striking colours of Firth Fell's flanks are a resplendent mixture of emerald and burnished gold, intermingled with bands of delicate grey. This mélange of ageless vegetation and rock attracts the eye as progress is made alongside the meandering Skirfare towards Hawkswick, which, along with other settlements within the dale, figured in the Doomesday Book.

The main road also provides fine views of Firth Fell as it progresses under the gaze of Hawkswick Clouder, a prominent limestone buttress, pock-marked with fissures and caves. The most notable of these is Dowkabottom Cave, which provided a dwelling place for early man until the fourth century A.D.

As Hawkswick approaches, Out Gang Lane leaves the main road to cross the tree-fringed river by means of a graceful stone bridge, beneath which dippers cavort and the Skirfare merrily dances. Beyond the bridge the lane meets the minor road, which follows the opposite riverbank, at the point where it enters the sheltered hamlet. An intriguing mixture of buildings, of varying ages, cluster around this narrow road as it winds between age-old walls, whose moss-encrusted stones evoke a feeling of constancy. In springtime swathes of exquisite blossom overhang these steadfast walls, adding a colourful dimension to a backdrop of weathered stone and russet-cloaked fellsides. Tiny mullioned windows bedeck the façade of a venerable cottage squatting in the shadow of an imposing three-storied house. The taller building stands out from its smaller neighbours, particularly because of its elegant Georgian windows.

Near the junction of Out Gang Lane and the main road lie two historic outposts. These are the Cotes, or farms, that were formerly granges belonging to Fountains Abbey. After the Norman Conquest Littondale became an extensive hunting forest within the estates owned by the Percys, a notable Northumberland family. The forest was given to the monks of Fountains by Richard Percy, with the exception of some sheep pastures already granted to Sawley Abbey. Several granges were established in the dale to aid control of the monastic estates. Washing and clipping of the Abbey's flock took place at Hawkswick and Arncliffe Cotes and there was probably a smithy at the latter. Traces of the original buildings remain to this day. The oldest structure is Hawkswick Cote's farmhouse that has been diligently restored.

Beyond these former granges looms the craggy face of Blue Scar, its higher reaches once a place of ancient habitation. A fine limestone pavement coats a broad ledge of the scar and indentations in this plateau provide evidence of prehistoric dwellings. As you pass beneath this eminent site, numerous cairns manifest themselves on its brooding crest.

During the short winter days, long shadows creep across the valley-floor as the sun begins to sink in a delicate blue amphitheatre. The snaking main road is plunged into virtual darkness as the rough hewn stone walls that bound it, mask its surface from the fleeting rays of the declining sun. At this time of year snow can be seen flecking the gaunt features of Blue Scar and the softer slopes of Firth Fell on the opposite side of the valley.

A journey through this part of the dale in summer provides a complete contrast, when a bright band of tarmac stretches towards Arncliffe, edged with lush green verges, strewn with colourful rashes of cranesbill and willow herb. A green carpet of pastureland spreads beneath a fringe of silvery limestone that glints in the strong sunlight. This landscape is a reminder that the valley has housed sweeping sheep ranges and provided rich grazing since the clearing of the primeval forests from its ample floor.

Inquisitive cattle peer over roadside walls, keenly watching passing vehicles and inviting sympathy for the conspicuous numbered tickets uncompromisingly clipped to their ears, to provide easy identification.

The triumphal entry into the 'hub' of Littondale, as Arncliffe can be described, is accomplished through an avenue of sycamore

Arncliffe

Arncliffe Church

View from Hesleden Gill

Foxup from Horsehead Moor

that leads towards the ample village green, which has remained largely unchanged for centuries. Several roads emanate from the centre of the village, including one that leads up-dale to Litton and Halton Gill. This thoroughfare crosses the Skirfare by means of sturdy Arncliffe Bridge, beyond which it is joined by the previously mentioned minor road that passes through Hawkswick.

If the latter road is chosen to reach Arncliffe, you will be rewarded by a journey that passes Hawkswick Wood, where, in springtime, the scent of lilies of the valley floats on the breeze and the plaintive cuckoo call can be heard, emanating from commandeered nests.

The two roads join forces, near Arncliffe Bridge, for the journey to Litton, the village from which the dale derives its name.

Arncliffe, however, is not a place to be treated summarily and is worth a little exploration. It is the only location in Littondale, with the exception of the lead-mines on its fringes, where significant industry was introduced. Arncliffe Mill, now converted into a row of cottages, was a corn mill during monastic times, owned by the canons of Bolton. At the end of the eighteenth century it was rebuilt, four stories high, for the manufacture of cotton. The top story has been removed since its closure in 1875 and it now provides an attractive group of dwellings that overlook the peaceful Cowside Beck.

In common with other Yorkshire Dales, hand spinning and weaving was carried out in many cottages throughout Littondale when the valley harboured a remote and self-contained community. Farming, however, has always been the mainstay of the dale and it has been supplemented over the years by toil in the harsh conditions of the lead-mines. In addition to the indigenous sheep, considerable stocks of deer were maintained, for hunting.

Arncliffe Church stands near Arncliffe Bridge, in an impressive setting, overlooking a broad sweep of the river. Its full title is the Church of St. Oswald with Halton Gill and it is currently the only church in the dale. Its extensive parish extends as far as Hubberholme, which lies in the adjacent valley of Langstrothdale.

The sturdy, rough-hewn tower is all that remains of the fifteenth-century version of this building, which has its origins in

Hawkswick

Saxon times. The attractive chancel screen was erected in the late nineteenth century to the memory of Archdeacon William Boyd, the 'Patriarch of the Dales.' He was vicar of Arncliffe for nearly sixty years and he carried out numerous alterations to the church during his stewardship. The shaping of much of the building into its present day form was performed in 1796 when everything except the tower was demolished and rebuilt in an unflattering style. Archdeacon Boyd gave the church a more ecclesiastical and religious character through his modifications.

Venture through the inviting lych-gate and you will pass through a churchyard carpeted with snowdrops during the harsh days of winter. The gate is also connected with an ancient rite, which was observed after wedding ceremonies at the church. This involved the happy couple being prevented from passing through the gate until they had handed coins over it, known as 'hensilver,' to the waiting men of the village.

One of the finest views of this compelling church is from Arncliffe Bridge, where it can be seen through a lattice-work of sycamore branches, which overlooks a series of mini cascades in the lively river. Boisterous chaffinch and vigilant nuthatch provide a

Halton Gill

sweet-sounding chorus, to augment this enchanting scene.

A notice, currently displayed in the entrance porch of the church, proudly proclaims that the parish is registered to plant a young yew, propagated from an ancient tree, estimated to be over 2000 years old, to celebrate the new millenium.

Close by the church stands a tiny school, still in use, its appeal enhanced by a steeply sloping roof and high-arched windows. Children from all parts of the valley attend this long-established school and they may learn during their studies of the legend concerning the witch of Littondale, who was reputed to have cast her spells in the vicinity. Her gullible clients were apparently sent to Arncliffe Bridge at midnight and whilst she performed her 'hocus pocus,' they would see their future revealed in the dark waters of the river.

Beside the bridge stands another interesting building, known as Bridge End House. It looks out over emerald lawns that roll to the riverside, a convenient setting for Charles Kingsley, who stayed there whilst researching the northern countryside for the atmosphere required in his projected novel, *The Water Babies*. The influence of the house and its location can be clearly perceived in that enduring book.

Arncliffe has another literary connection, with no less a person than William Wordsworth. His poem, *The White Doe of Rylstone,* describes the dale as 'Amerdale' and the village hall bears this name. A further reference to the poem is provided by the name Amerdale Dub, which lies at the confluence of the Skirfare and the Wharfe.

The centrepiece of Arncliffe's village green is the stone pump that formerly quenched the thirst of the villagers. It now stands dormant, a relic of a quieter and more unhurried era. The pump's rusting mechanism may have succumbed to the ravages of time and use, but its stonework remains a delight to the eye.

At one corner of the green stands the Falcon Hotel, an inn of long-standing and another place for quenching the thirst. A former host was Marmaduke Miller, an accomplished wood engraver and artist, who died in 1970. It has a reputation for hospitality to travellers, who trod the old track from Malham, known as Monks' Road, which descends into the dale along the steep slopes above the Cowside Beck and passes the door of the inn. Unfortunately present-day hospitality does not appear to extend to passing walkers, for recently an unwelcome notice was displayed outside that declared, 'Do not bring your muddy boots in here, this is not the Pennine Way!'

When the Yorkshire Television series, *Emmerdale* was starting life as *Emmerdale Farm,* Arncliffe was portrayed as the original village and the Falcon Hotel became the first 'Woolpack.'

As the village green is approached, a road sign indicates that Settle and Malham can be reached. If the road which bisects the green is followed through the village, it changes course just beyond and climbs along the northern crest of the valley of the Cowside Beck, as a prelude to a scenic journey to Malham that lies nine miles away.

The road leading to Settle is the one that crosses Arncliffe Bridge and heads for Litton. On this section of its journey through the dale, a cottage bearing the name 'Dalegarth' is passed. It is a reminder of the occupation of the dale by Norsemen, for 'garth' was their word for an opening, gap, or enclosure and it features prominently in this valley.

As an alternative to the road that runs through the valley there is a good selection of riverside and meadowland paths that traverse the dale. The section from Arncliffe to Litton is typical of the invigorating walks that these paths provide. Stout footwear is recommended, particularly in winter, for the valley-floor can become saturated and very muddy in parts. Do not let this possibility inhibit you, for the rewards are significant. You will be surrounded by some of the finest scenery and flora in the Dales. Emerald pastures and limestone fell sides, scoured by the elements, form a memorable landscape that is patterned with the familiar network of ancient stone walls and flecked with stone barns. How well the craftsmen of bygone years constructed the innumerable miles of drystone enclosure and the receptacles for hay and livestock, many of which have their origins in the seventeenth century. In contrast to the barns, of which a proportion are sadly decaying, the drystone walls, some rising at improbable angles, remain in remarkable condition, and are a tribute to the present day renovators, who continue the age-old craft.

Sheep graze the lower pastures in the colder months and these hungry animals ensure that the fields are close-cropped. Despite these wooly lawn mowers, stitchwort and dog violets exhibit themselves in springtime. At this time of year the slopes are alive with primula. Rosettes of draba, or whitlow grass, litter the nooks and crannies of the barer rock faces. Other lime-loving plants such as rock rose, milkwort and harts tongue fern add to the profusion of plants that characterise this quiet dale.

Not content with keeping the green carpet of the valley-floor under control, the ravenous sheep hurry towards walkers as they traverse the meadows in winter expecting a supply of fodder, normally provided by the farmer. As you dash their hopes and pass them by, their disdainful stares accompany you to the next stile.

Scoska Wood, maintained and preserved by English Nature, coats the southern fellsides in this section of the valley. These delicate woods, which soar above the lush meadows, represent the largest concentration of ash and rowan in the Dales.

Beneath their gaze the path hugs the riverside, passing lines of ancient, gnarled trees, whose lichen-smothered branches weave intricate patterns. Contorted roots litter the path, eager to trap unwary feet. They burrow beneath nearby walls, in their efforts to escape the confines of the riverbank.

The white-walled Queens Arms signifies the approach of Litton and this hostelry is clearly visible from road or field path. It stands at the spot where the old road from Settle crosses the dale road, prior to climbing Firth Fell and descending to Buckden, in Wharfedale. This green track presents a steep and strenuous ascent to the watershed, but the visual rewards offer ample compensation. A bird's eye view of the village unfolds as the slope becomes more testing. Its huddle of stone cottages can be seen, issuing gentle streams of smoke from their chimneys. As the elusive crest is approached, sympathy can be felt for the monks and packmen that negotiated this tortuous route in all weathers.

The river was crossed in earlier times by a ford, which still exists, and a bridle track, part of the former Settle to Buckden road, runs from it to join the dale road near the Queens Arms.

Litton has an abundance of paths that surround the river and its current crossing point is a narrow wooden footbridge lying in the shadow of an attractive row of mellow stone cottages. A series of shallow, but vigorous, waterfalls punctuate the Skirfare as it approaches the bridge under the gaze of these timeless dwellings and their decorative gardens. The date 1707 is visible on one of the door-heads of the cottages and, despite their great age, these buildings appear just as solid and appealing as they must have done during their infancy.

Litton proudly displays its great age by means of several other dates visible above cottage doorways. One such abode overlooks the tiny village green, on whose perimeter stands a seat, surrounded by bowers of rowan, which bears the inscription 'Rest awhile in lovely Litton.'

Nearby stands a large and intriguing block of stone with an eyelet sunk into its top. One can only guess at its purpose.

A little way down the road from the green, Manor Cottage occupies the site of the original manor house, whose origins are early nineteenth-century.

Beyond Litton, road and field path travel up the dale towards Nether Hesleden and Halton Gill. Hillsides begin to close in and the valley narrows appreciably. The barrier of Horsehead Moor comes into view, a great bulkhead that terminates the dale.

Nether Hesleden shelters in a comforting fold in the valley-side, at the foot of Hesleden Gill. As the gill is approached the distant hump of Plover Hill dominates its head, closely followed by its neighbour, Penyghent. Ancient cultivation terraces cloak the fellsides at the mouth of the gill. These obsolete, grass-coated ledges gaze down upon the present day farm, whose agricultural methods are much more advanced. Cottages, of long-standing, make up this tiny settlement, which, after the Dissolution, was inhabited by yeomen farmers, who inherited much of the dale in the succeeding centuries.

At the end of the monastic era the Cliffords of Skipton Castle acquired most of the lands through marriage with the Percys and by purchase. Eventually the dale was transferred to the yeomanry, who shaped it into the landscape of today.

Little has altered in Nether Hesleden since the eighteenth century, apart from the appearance of a commemorative stone in front of one of the buildings that bears the inscription, 'To Diana, Queen of Hearts,' a recent tribute to her memory.

The upper reaches of Hesleden Gill contain a fine limestone pavement that nestles beneath the shapely backdrop of Penyghent and Fountains Fell. These prominent landmarks lie on opposite sides of quiet Silverdale, through which passes the scenic road from Halton Gill to Stainforth and Settle. It crosses the Pennine Way at Dalehead, the former site of a packhorse inn. Where road and long distance footpath meet, stands a large weathered stone, the base of Ulfgil Cross, a boundary stone of the former lands of Fountains Abbey. At this point the Pennine Way has descended Fountains Fell and is about to tackle the heights of Penyghent as it heads for Horton-in-Ribblesdale.

The name Fountains Fell recalls the time when the surrounding lands were part of the vast estates, owned by the monks of Fountains, which stretched into the north of the Lake District.

A sign at Nether Hesleden Indicates that Foxup and Cosh can be reached by footpath. The accompanying dale road travels to Halton Gill, alongside the River Skirfare, which writhes energetically through luxuriant pastureland.

To walk the field paths to Foxup is a journey to be savoured. The feeling of being at one with nature pervades an amphitheatre of delight. Crumpled fellsides, with wild crests, overlook your every move and several copses fleck the surrounding meadows. Beyond Hesleden Gill the slopes of the Berghs rise from the valley floor.

Blue Scar

These ragged limestone heights are a rabbit warren of pot-holes and caves, many with intriguing names, such as Flamethrower Hole, Red Dot Pots and Calena Pot. Hesleden Bergh, High and Low Berghs, still bearing evidence of former Iron Age settlements, shadow your progress towards the head of the dale.

Across the valley huddles Halton Gill, embedded in the base of a cleft in rippling hillsides that cry out for a giant iron to smooth their tawny faces. The village needs all the protection available from the harsh winds that buffet its isolated setting.

Clearly in view above Halton Gill, a scar lacerates the slopes of Horsehead Moor. It is the tentative beginnings of the ancient track that links the head of Littondale with the hamlets of Langstrothdale. High above the village the rutted thoroughfare diverges, one branch heading over the Horsehead Pass for Yockenthwaite, the other towards Beckermonds, where the Greenfield Beck and the Oughtershaw Beck meet to form the River Wharfe.

These tracks were in use during the time of the Bronze Age traders. In later years they were trod by drovers and packmen, who

The head of Hesleden Gill

battled with rough terrain and fierce winds in the daunting upland habitat of curlew and ring ouzel. They form part of one of the early routes through the Pennines and provide a clue to the origin of Halton Gill's name, the 'halt on the gill.'

The cluster of stone buildings that comprise this compact settlement appear unaffected by the passing centuries, apart from the occasional intrusion of modern farm sheds. In former times Halton Gill was virtually self sufficient, boasting its own tiny church, which also acted as the local school. This seventeenth-century edifice still stands by the roadside, but is currently known as Church House, having been converted into a private dwelling. Children now make a journey down the dale to Arncliffe for lessons. There is a bus service that reaches Halton Gill twice a day, a vast improvement on earlier times when the only mode of transport was the horse or 'Shanks's pony.'

An impressive hall overlooks the village. The well-maintained building was erected, in 1641, by the Dawson family, which still occupies Langcliffe Hall, in Ribblesdale. The monks of Fountains built an early church here and also provided other amenities for the area, such as a hospice at Litton. This reveals that the monks sowed as well as reaped. They derived revenue from the dale by digging for lead and silver and they also used its pastures for grazing their sheep. In return they provided the dale's families with work and firm religious foundations.

A bunk barn is available for walkers at Halton Gill. It provides ample, but inexpensive accommodation in a splendid rural setting. All facets of country life can be encountered in this close knit community, including the age-old skill of rounding up sheep. The shrill whistle of the shepherd floats on the air as his faithful dogs alternately scamper, or remain motionless and watchful, whilst the sheep are controlled and driven in the required direction. Pheasants can be seen cantering through fields and gardens. These witless birds appear to have an aversion to flying, for whenever they are approached they run away like naughty children.

At the entrance to the village the dale road veers to the south-west for its journey to Stainforth and Settle. From this point a narrow finger of tarmac, less than a mile in length extends to the head of the dale. This serves the last settlement of any size in the valley, Foxup, which shelters at the foot of the Foxup Beck.

The road branch terminates at Foxup Bridge, where the Cosh Beck and the Foxup Beck mingle to give birth to the River Skirfare.

A pleasant field path links Halton Gill and Foxup amidst surroundings that become increasingly remote, with the exception of an unusual pattern of fields, visible on the hillside beyond Foxup. Linked by an intricate series of drystone walls, these hill pastures present an incongruous collection of inter-locking green wedges.

Foxup is a hamlet consisting of large, well-appointed farms and trim cottages that have replaced the remains of four older properties. Its history is not forgotten for the initials 'M.K.' can still be seen above the door of one of the farmhouses, which illustrate its connection with the Knowles family, an old Littondale dynasty.

The hamlet comprises two adjacent communities. The first of these, a row of three farms, squats near the bridge. A short journey along the lane that winds alongside the Foxup Beck exposes a second group of neat stone buildings sheltering in a tree-lined cleft at the foot of Low Bergh. Here the beck tumbles between rounded slopes, which house numerous enclosures bearing time-honoured names, such as Parrock Hill, Scutching Close and Tommy's Croft Laithe that stir the imagination.

One of the finest views of Foxup can be enjoyed from the track that scales Horsehead Moor above Halton Gill. This vantage-point reveals the shapely channel that climbs beyond the village into the high moorland under the distant gaze of the distinctive summit of Ingleborough.

A green track, known as Foxup Road, can be seen rising steeply from the village onto the flank of Low Berg, from where it contours the slopes of Foxup Moor to disappear into a landscape of ling and rough pasture. This ancient thoroughfare eventually joins the Pennine Way, at the foot of Penyghent.

The isolated outpost of Cosh, sequestered high amongst the bleak moorland of the valley head, had remained an intriguing and unvisited spot for me, until recently, when I decided to discover if this former site of a remote grange, for Fountains Abbey, was inhabited. There were three dwellings in this tiny colony at one time. The inhabitants, out of necessity, were industrious and self-sufficient and, like many other cottages in the dale in former times, they hand spun and wove cloth, to make their own clothes.

In 1953 the farm, the last building to be occupied, was abandoned and left to the ravages of the elements. The incumbents, the Brown family, literally lived in a world of their own. Mrs. Brown frequently invited passing walkers into the farmhouse for a cup of tea and a chat. This was her way of discovering the happenings in the outside world. Two of her girls lodged at Halton Gill from Monday to Friday to save a daily round trip of six miles to school. William Brown and his family thought nothing of walking five miles to Horton-in-Ribblesdale to catch a train, or of driving some of their Swaledale sheep the ten miles to market at Hawes. A supply of food was collected each month, by horse and cart, from Foxup, where it was left by a grocer from Hebden. Coal was carted, five hundredweights at a time, from Grassington railway station, twenty-five miles away. As this was no easy matter the Browns resorted to digging peat from the surrounding moorland.

Church House, Halton Gill

I set out from Foxup, eager to discover what had become of this little corner of no-man's land. My quest began as I joined an exceedingly rough and messy track that snaked into the hills beyond the sign that indicates it is two miles to Cosh, or 'Kosh,' as it was originally named by the Norsemen who settled in the higher reaches of the Dales. The track climbs alongside the lively Cosh Beck into a wild landscape swept by keen and inhospitable winds. It is the unfrequented territory of the lapwing and redshank, who are wary of intruders.

Eyes straining for signs of habitation, I battled with the gradient and the atrocious conditions underfoot. There is an alternative path that contours the slopes of Harrop Barns, which lies on the far side of the beck. This offers better access, but requires an eventual crossing of the watercourse, which is no easy task when it is in spate.

The terrain appeared bleak and daunting on that harsh winter afternoon, but in the late spring it is enhanced by hoar rocks that are aflame with primrose and hyacinth, which spread tiny patches of blue beneath thickets of hazel scrub.

The farm at Cosh

I felt like a lonely shepherd roaming this wild countryside in search of his flock and it was easy to imagine the canting of ancient sheep numerals, which they used for counting their charges. 'Een, teen, tethera' could almost be heard resonating through the empty landscape.

Trying to increase my pace, I merely managed to slither on the unremitting surface of the stubborn track, which climbed remorselessly as far as the eye could see. As I bowed my head in the face of the stiffening wind, I noticed tyre-marks embedded in it. My hopes were raised, because this indicated that vehicles, probably of the four-wheeled variety, were obviously using this route.

As I laboured higher into the hills, there was strangely no sign of my objective. Had all trace of Cosh disappeared, I wondered? If so, where did those tyre-tracks lead?

Suddenly all was revealed as I reached a small hollow in the hillside. A tiny croft appeared, without warning, within this hidden and sheltered haven, taking me completely by surprise. Despite the tiny farmhouse being in a good state of repair, the place possessed an air of decay. Crumbling stone dominated the scene. Remnants of drystone walls and the gaunt ruins of an old farmhouse were scattered beneath a windswept canvas of rugged moorland and angry sky. I half-expected Heathcliff to appear in the midst of this stark scenario. If there was a lonelier place in the Yorkshire Dales, I had yet to find it.

The sight of two Land Rovers parked by the croft jerked me back to reality. There was, however, no sign of activity. The white paintwork of the recently extended croft shone like a beacon in the gloomy oasis, suggesting habitation. However, the lack of smoke from the chimneys and the absence of curtains at the windows did not bear this out.

I understood that the surrounding land was maintained by the farmer at High Birkwith, in nearby Ribblesdale, and I reasoned that the vehicles and the sheep possibly belonged to him. I scanned my surroundings for signs of life, but found none. Reluctantly I left the intriguing setting, my expectations unfulfilled. The light was already beginning to fade on that gloomy winter's afternoon and a return journey of several miles awaited me.

As I hurriedly returned along the inhospitable track I pondered the intriguing fact that this beautiful and secluded dale had not divulged the secret of its wild and untamed upper reaches. This demonstrates that every Yorkshire Dale retains a certain air of mystery, which contributes towards its unique character.

CHAPTER FIVE

I Took the Blows

My Way, the popular song immortalised by Frank Sinatra, could have been written for Brian Close. This gifted, all-round sportsman received many physical and mental buffetings during his colourful career, which were meted out by cricket balls, footballers, cricket committees and the MCC, to name but a few.

An open and honest man, he has certainly done things his way, without fear or favour; a characteristic that, in particular, did not endear him to cricket's administrators. He staunchly believes that the only way to play a game is to win. Not by fair means or foul, but through maximum effort and dedication. To put it bluntly, he hates to lose.

He played sport like a true Yorkshireman, hard, but fair. Yet under that steely exterior lies a sensitivity that has surfaced on several occasions. When confronted with some of life's hard knocks, he openly admits that he has not been afraid to show emotion. One such occurrence, when he was removed from the captaincy of Yorkshire, so upset him that he was reduced to tears. Worse than the pain of losing a job that he cherished, was the belief that his removal was undeserved.

Also, his gritty persona hides an innate kindness, a trait suitably demonstrated by the encouragement and guidance that he gave to the young cricketers under his stewardship at Yorkshire County Cricket Club. He was also involved in the development of budding talent whilst captaining Somerset and it gave him immense satisfaction to have played a part in giving some truly great players to the game.

An assertive jut of the jaw and a determined glint of the eye provide a striking resemblance to the wartime fighter ace, Douglas Bader, who was an equally resolute character. If Brian had suffered the misfortune endured by his alter ego, I could imagine him stomping to the crease for Yorkshire on a pair of tin legs, considering it nothing out of the ordinary.

Brian was weaned on cricket, following in the footsteps of his father and grandfather, who both played for local clubs. Although

Brian Close

he never saw his grandfather in action, he played alongside his father, who was a wicket keeper-batsman for East Leeds.

His rise through cricket's junior ranks was meteoric. He played for Rawdon first team at the tender age of eleven. The memory of his first game for them is undiminished. His debut was against Menston, where he scored nine runs and took two wickets for twenty. He still wonders what his opponents felt like when confronted with a mere child.

At seventeen he was playing for Yeadon, in the Bradford League and by the end of that particular season he had been picked for the Yorkshire second team. The following year he was invited to play for the county, (at that time one had to wait for an invitation) on a southern tour that included matches against Cambridge University, Oxford University and Somerset. His first match was against Cambridge, at Fenners, and it also marked the first team baptism of Fred Tueman and Frank Lowson. Brian performed well enough in the matches against the university teams to retain a place in the side for his first championship game, against Somerset.

His life might have taken a different course if he had taken the advice of his headmaster at Aireborough Grammar School. Brian had achieved good results in his Higher School Certificate exams, with passes in mathematics, physics, chemistry and biology and he was advised to go to Cambridge to read the former. Good at science and poor at arts, he developed a desire to study medicine, with the aim of becoming a doctor, before a full time cricket career beckoned.

At the time of his departure from school, aged seventeen and a half, most university places had been filled with people whose education had been interrupted by the Second World War. Consequently, Brian went into the army six months later, having obtained provisional university acceptance upon completion of his term of National Service. His call up was delayed due to his appearance for the medical nursing a football injury. He had been on Leeds United's books since he was fourteen and had already played for the England Youth XI. A month or two was allowed for his recovery, before reporting for duty and this period was subsequently extended.

During the intervening months he capitalised on his all-round

Brian aged seventeen, with the West Riding FA Youth XI

sporting prowess by signing professional forms for Leeds United and, when the cricket season began, earned another invitation to play for Yorkshire. The world was apparently at his feet and he seemed set to emulate his idol, Dennis Compton, who was playing cricket for England and professional football for Arsenal.

As it transpired, university did not materialise and by the age of twenty-two his football career had been tragically ended due to a clutch of serious injuries. One of these was suffered during a clash with Ted Robledo, who played alongside his brother George for Newcastle United, which so badly damaged Brian's thigh that he spent several months in hospital.

His early promise at Leeds had resulted in his signing for Arsenal, but unfortunately his twin commitments of football and cricket proved too much for the illustrious London club and he was given a free transfer. He joined Bradford City and everything went well until a game against Port Vale when he injured his knee. What was at first thought to be ligament damage, proved to be a torn

Brian with Yorkshire CCC (1949).

cartilage that required an operation. Although he put every effort into getting fit once more and played for the reserve team after an absence of five weeks, the knee could not stand the strain and it kept him out of sport for eighteen months.

This was a devastating blow to an aspiring young sportsman and he decided to concentrate on cricket and win his place back in the Yorkshire side. A further setback followed when, having achieved this, he developed problems with his batting. He was suffering severe headaches and blurred vision and became so worried that he became afraid to play for fear of failing. Things came to a head when he went out to field as substitute in a match against Middlesex, at Lords and muffed a couple of straightforward stops. The Yorkshire captain, Norman Yardley, sent him to hospital, where he was given a thorough examination and told that he had been having migraine attacks.

Brian returned to the ground with his mind in turmoil. Could he beat this new adversary? Was he exaggerating its effects? Was he just a coward, unable to deal with a loss of form and incapable of overcoming it? Would he ever return to those carefree times when he played for the sheer joy of being involved in top-class cricket?

The understanding Norman Yardley, sensing Brian's dilemma, gave him a choice before the next game against Somerset. He could either accompany the team to Taunton, or go home and rest. He chose to give it one more try and went to Somerset. His mood of despair was slightly lifted during Yorkshire's first innings when he scored thirty runs and was, in his view, unjustifiably run out.

After Somerset's second innings, Brian was still brooding over the unfair run out decision and bemoaning the fact that nothing ever went right for very long. At five minutes notice, he was unexpectedly instructed by the captain to open the batting for Yorkshire's second innings. There was no time to worry about batting in a strange position, no time to wonder if his eyes would give him trouble and no time to ponder on his recent series of low scores. In a flurry of activity, he changed back into his whites, put on his pads and hurried from the pavilion. Set 284 to win, Yorkshire achieved this target for the loss of only two wickets. Top scorer was Brian with 143, a resounding century that put him firmly on the road to recovery.

Following this success he continued to open the batting for Yorkshire and five weeks later he was selected to open for England against South Africa. Brian scored the highest number of runs in the first innings, helping England to win the match and clinch the test series. He was still troubled by migraine, but once it had been diagnosed and success had returned, the condition was easier to control. Another important factor was that Brian's belief in himself had been restored and he remains eternally grateful to Norman Yardley for his understanding and perceptiveness.

Life felt good once more, for Brian had climbed back from the abyss and returned to the pinnacle of cricket success, a position he had attained, some years earlier, at the age of nineteen. He had been selected for the England tour of Australia and New Zealand in the company of test players who had been schoolboy idols. Len Hutton, Cyril Washbrook, Dennis Compton and Freddie Brown were in the party that sailed for Australia in October 1950 and

Brian had to pinch himself, when the team departed, to make sure that it was not merely a dream.

Brian was still doing his National Service at this time and was granted six months leave to go on the tour. This was no real hardship as far as the army was concerned, for he had never had a job throughout his term. Their view was that, as he was away so often, playing football or cricket, it would be a waste of time to intervene.

The tour was an experience, in more ways than one. He departed a naive boy and came back a man. So in awe was he of the senior players that he was frightened to approach, or even talk to them. His attitude was interpreted as anti-social and arrogant. Consequently, he became isolated from the older players and had to rely on the companionship of some of the younger members of the touring party, such as his room-mate, Gilbert Parkinson and Bob Berry. From his idols he received a wall of indifference that developed into hostility. This was tragic, for Brian was longing for any one of them to take him to one side and offer a little encouragement and advice.

A run of poor performances and a nagging groin injury compounded his plight and by the time the team went to Tasmania, for a mid-tour series of matches, he was beginning to feel like a leper. Despite his visit to a specialist, in Hobart, for an examination of his injury, the captain for the Tasmanian section of the tour, Dennis Compton, believed that he was malingering. When he showed Compton the letter of diagnosis from the specialist, it was torn up and its contents ignored. The medical report recommended that Brian had three to four weeks' rest, to allow the ruptured roots of a tendon to heal. He was informed by his irate captain that he would be playing in the next match and he was forced to carry on playing in further matches, with the injury getting worse.

They returned to Australia and Brian, playing in his fifth game since being told that his injury would take time to heal, was in serious trouble. His leg was dragging as he ran and after bowling four overs, he felt something snap. Collapsing in a heap, he had to be carried from the field. For the rest of the day he lay on a table, sick and feverish, with ice-packs being applied to his head. At the end of that ordeal, the senior players gave him a thorough cursing.

Brian in action

Brian grew up on that tour. He learnt invaluable lessons that helped him during his years of captaincy. There were times, he realised, when a player needs to be left alone, times when he needs encouragement, times when he needs guidance and times when he needs a roasting.

In retrospect he can even sympathise with the attitude of the senior professionals on that fateful tour. Some had lost several years of cricketing life through the Second World War and realised that their trip to Australia may have been their last. It was such a wonderful country to visit, virtually unaffected by the war and rationing. Consequently, they wanted enjoyment, not saddling with inexperienced youngsters, who needed discipline, advice and encouragement.

On his return to England, Brian discovered that during his absence, the term of National Service had been increased from eighteen months to two years, which meant that he had another six months to serve. He reported back to Catterick and the following summer he threw himself into re-establishing his cricketing credentials. He scored an abundance of runs, including several centuries, one against the South African tourists, which provided some consolation for the miseries of the Australian tour.

For the next decade his cricket career prospered. He enjoyed playing for a Yorkshire side that had tremendous ability, but found honours hard to achieve. They languished in the shadow of the great Surrey team, which included the renowned Bedser twins, Jim Laker and Tony Lock. The county championship virtually became Surrey's property during the nineteen-fifties; they held it for seven consecutive seasons during that decade.

Brian was a keen student of the game and never missed an opportunity to learn, or to involve himself in the tactical side of cricket. As his leadership ability developed he moved through the ranks to senior professional and endeavoured to give his captain maximum support and sometimes, unwelcome advice!

During this period Brian served under several Yorkshire captains. He retains the utmost respect for the first of them, Norman Yardley, who retired in 1955. Until he himself was appointed captain in 1963 he played under the leadership of a further three.

Billy Sutcliffe succeeded Norman Yardley. He was the son of the legendary Herbert Sutcliffe, who had christened him William

Herbert Hobbs Sutcliffe, quite a name to live up to.

Unfortunately Billy was unable to do so, preferring to be 'one of the lads' rather than a leader. Unable to exert much influence over the team, his position was also undermined by his inflexible approach and pre-conceived ideas of how each day's play should be conducted.

Billy departed after two seasons, to be replaced by Ronnie Burnet, an amateur, like his predecessors. This was the era of the professional and amateur cricketer and the Yorkshire committee preferred the latter as captain. Ronnie was a good, likeable man, but he also struggled to control a team of tough, experienced players, with strong personalities. However, he survived his first season and during his second in charge, Yorkshire won the championship, for which he deserves credit.

In 1960 Vic Wilson became captain. He was a sound player, a prolific scorer of runs and an excellent close-fielder. It was a magnificent team that he inherited, but Vic seemed unsure how to guide it to greater heights. A quiet man, somewhat introverted, he appeared to lack the vision and tactical strengths required for success. He relied heavily on Fred Trueman, who he would almost bowl into the ground on numerous occasions, irrespective of the conditions, the state of the pitch, or the abilities of the opposition. Despite his limitations, he had a successful period of leadership, for during two of his three seasons in charge, the team won the championship.

Brian had the good fortune to deputise as captain on one occasion during Vic's first year as leader. It was against Derbyshire, at Chesterfield, and he found it a tremendous thrill. Despite failing to score in the first innings, he wasn't nervous about being in charge and Yorkshire eventually won the match by fifty-eight runs. Brian had been confident in his tactical knowledge and he enjoyed putting his own ideas to the test.

He did, however, suffer one embarrassment during the match, when he discovered that he hated walking out onto the field at the head of his team. It gave him an uneasy feeling and ever since that occasion he always slowed down as he left the pavilion to allow the next player to catch up.

In 1963 Brian's chance came and he was appointed captain of Yorkshire. It turned out to be a wonderful summer. The team won the championship once again, in spite of numerous Test

Tong Park Dam, Baildon

Ilkley

Middleham

Brian and Sir Garfield Sobers

appearances by several senior players. He enjoyed the challenge of some great matches, free from his previous frustrations and able to follow his own instincts. His sole objective was winning, but I am sure that he did not go to the extreme of the old Yorkshire player, Emmott Robinson. In the early days of Roses matches with their rivals, Lancashire, Emmott reputedly used to say 'Ah do?' to the opposition on the first morning, then nothing but 'How's that?' for the remainder of the game.

Under his leadership, Yorkshire thrived for the next eight seasons, winning the championship four times and the Gillette Cup twice. He proved a great tactician with splendid flair and success with his county brought further rewards at Test level. Having played for England on several occasions, he was appointed captain in 1966 and 1967.

During his captaincy the national side never lost a Test, an outstanding record. He enjoyed being England's captain and doing a job well, because it brought prestige to his country, his family and himself. Success, however, did not prevent his untimely removal from the highest position in the game, which struck right into every professional instinct that he possesses.

With six victories and one draw from his matches in charge, he fully expected to retain his position for the forthcoming tour of the West Indies, in the autumn of 1967. During the series against Pakistan that summer he had a feeling that something was not quite right when he was pressured to bring back Colin Cowdrey for the second Test. Brian felt that a change in the team was unjustified and he expressed his views accordingly. Call it a premonition, but from then on he felt that there was something in the air.

His fears were increased when a well-known cricket correspondent for a national newspaper warned him to keep his nose clean, as the MCC were looking for a chance to replace him. At just the time when he needed to avoid controversy, he became embroiled in two incidents that were to seal his fate.

They occurred at Edgbaston, in August, when Yorkshire needed to beat Warwickshire to go to the top of the championship table. Their opponents bowled well and Yorkshire were dismissed for 238 in their first innings. When Warwickshire batted, several chances were missed in the field and the bowling was pretty poor. At lunchtime, Brian led his team into the pavilion, deep in thought about what to say to his players during the break. Unfortunately, as he did so, he heard a very unpleasant remark directed at him from the Warwickshire members' seats. Normally such a comment would have been ignored, but Brian was hot, worried and short-tempered. He approached the man whom he thought had uttered the remark, placed his hand on his shoulder and asked politely if he had. The man replied that he had not. Brian apologised and went in to lunch, assuming that the incident would be quickly forgotten.

The match progressed and Yorkshire did not make up ground in their second innings, leaving Warwickshire requiring only 145 to win. In Brian's view it was up to his team to make them fight for every run. Unfortunately this rearguard action was to cost him the England captaincy.

At no time during Warwickshire's innings did Brian instruct his bowlers to take their time about bowling their overs, but due to the weather conditions, the ball had to be frequently dried, which caused delay. Bowlers were required to wipe the ball under the supervision of the umpire, but Yorkshire's faster bowlers carried a cloth in their pockets to save time by drying the ball as they made their way back to their marks. Despite this aid, other, uncontrollable factors intervened and a slow over rate ensued.

The game was eventually drawn and when Brian shook hands with Warwickshire's captain, Mike Smith, he explained that Yorkshire had to make them fight all the way. To his credit the opposing captain replied that he fully understood their approach.

Brian thought that was the end of the situation, but it was to have dire consequences. On the following Wednesday he was called to Lords to face a panel of former county captains in order to answer complaints regarding his team's tactics against Warwickshire. Despite his prior presentation of a full and honest written report on the alleged time-wasting and his belief that his actions had been correct, the verdict was a stunning blow.

The panel concluded that delaying tactics had been used, which constituted unfair play and were against the best interests of the game. Brian Close, as captain, was held entirely responsible and was severely censured.

The situation was unbelievable and Brian was livid. His first thought was, 'How can I captain a team after this?' It was an awful dilemma because he was due to lead England on the following day.

He felt like telling the powers-that-be to find a new captain, but was persuaded not to do so by Brian Sellers, chairman of Yorkshire CCC, who had attended the inquiry as an observer.

Brian led England at the Oval next day with his mind in turmoil, but the team and the crowd were magnificent, with no mention being made at all regarding the Lord's verdict. The nagging fear that he was about to lose the England captaincy had crept upon him and his anxiety was not relieved by what happened next.

Two days later he was approached to make a statement about a story that was due to appear in *The People* next day, with the accompanying headline: 'Brian Close Sensation. He Attacked Man in Crowd.' This was another body-blow that appeared just at the time when the captaincy for the West Indies tour was being discussed by the selectors.

Newspaper reporters swarmed around the England team's hotel that Sunday evening when Brian and his wife, Vivienne, returned from Ken Barrington's home, where they had been staying, in order to avoid them. Vivienne entered the hotel by the front door, but Brian, who had been advised not to make any statements to the press, furtively sneaked in by the rear entrance. It was not a very dignified situation for an England captain, particularly when he was trying to win a Test match and with it, the series.

England did triumph, but Brian did not escape the inevitable outcome. The first hint of the fateful news came from the Pakistan captain, Hanif, who whispered to him in the Oval pavilion, ' I have heard rumours that they haven't picked you for the West Indies.' When Brian replied that it was the first he had heard about the decision, Hanif added, 'I sincerely hope that you get the captaincy.'

Half an hour later he was officially informed by the chairman of selectors, Doug Insole, that he would not be leading the side in the West Indies. Immediately after this shattering news Brian had to attend the post-match reception, where he was required to make a speech, smile at people and make polite conversation. All the time he was bleeding inside. He may not bruise easily, but he does bleed.

His reputation for hardness and resistance to bruising was acquired through the numerous blows from cricket balls that he received during his career. He took more than his share of stick

Brian Close CBE – with his family at Buckingham Palace, 1975

from West Indian fast bowlers, particularly Wes Hall and Charlie Griffiths, who were in their prime when Brian had the temerity to advance down the wicket whilst facing their thunderbolts. He adopted these tactics during one game in order to speed things up and force a result. There had been many delays during the match due to rain and bad light and Brian sensed that time was running out. His other motive was to upset Wes Hall, thereby destroying his bowling rhythm. Brian reasoned that it would be very difficult for his opponents to get him out, as there was no chance of being dismissed leg before wicket.

Taking such blows that would have turned you and I into quivering wrecks was all in a day's work to Brian and there were several incidents throughout his career when he brushed aside the most fearful of hits. Some of these are highlighted in his autobiography *I Don't Bruise Easily,* written in association with Don Mosey.

One incident, which became an anecdote for many after-dinner speakers, concerned Brian's frequent spells of fielding at suicidal positions close to the bat. During a county match against Gloucestershire, a batsman hit a ball onto his forehead and it rebounded into the hands of his teammate, Phillip Sharpe, who gratefully accepted the catch. At Gravesend, against Kent, Brian took a blow on the head from a full-blooded clout by a big-hitting batsman and the ball flew towards the boundary, stopping just short of the line.

During the final stage of another match, at Hull, Younis Ahmed drove a juicy half-volley from Yorkshire's Don Wilson straight at Brian and the ball thumped him on the shin. It was very painful and he hopped a bit, but he was ready for the next ball, which was late coming. Brian turned and shouted to Don Wilson to get on with it, as there were not many overs left to force a win, but Don was staring at the blood seeping through his flannels and trickling into his boot. Brian insisted that they got on with things and that he would seek medical assistance later, so the game carried on.

These occurrences appear in a chapter with the cryptic title 'Blood and Teas.' The 'blood' is self-explanatory and the 'teas' refers to Brian's penchant for the beverage, which is his favourite drink when he is really thirsty. 'Closey's pot of tea,' in the dressing room, became a standard requirement on all county grounds by the time he retired from first-class cricket. He had been persuasive enough to train the groundstaff at the various venues to brew it to his liking.

Whilst playing in South Africa with Derek Robbins' touring side, he developed the ritual a little further by having a teapot and cup brought to him on the pitch during the drinks interval. This idea caught on with other players in the side, but was not continued upon their return to England.

The hardest blow of Brian's life came on the 25 November 1970. It was much worse than those from cricket balls and even more severe than the loss of the England captaincy, three years earlier.

Out of the blue came a request from the Yorkshire secretary to go to county headquarters at Headingley that morning and no further explanation was given. It was a surprise to find no committee in session when he arrived, only Mr. Nash, the secretary and Brian Sellars, the embodiment of Yorkshire cricket, who had led the splendid county team of the 1930's and was now the club's chairman.

Brian was taken aback when Mr. Sellers said, 'Well Brian, you have had a good innings,' but he was completely unprepared for what followed. The chairman told him that the committee had met and decided that his services were no longer required. There and then, Brian was asked to make the choice between resignation and being sacked.

Dazed by this bombshell, Brian said weakly, 'How long have I got to decide because I would like a word with my wife?' The reply was 'Ten minutes.' He was told that he had to decide before leaving the room and that two statements had already been prepared for a public announcement and his decision would determine which of them was issued. Everything was cut and dried.

Brian struggled to think rationally and after some deliberation, blurted out that he would resign. This appeared at the time to be the most dignified exit. As soon as he uttered those words the tension went out of the chairman and the secretary. He realised that he had taken the pressure off them, but none from himself. All he wanted to do was get out of Headingley and talk to Vivienne, who had given him tremendous support through all his previous tribulations.

Driving home, his mind was in a whirl and he wanted to cry. As he progressed along Kirkstall road his eyes misted up so much that he had to stop the car. He got out and was promptly sick at the side of the road.

When he arrived home his wife was out, collecting their daughter from school. On her return she asked what on earth was the matter. She could obviously tell by his expression that something was radically wrong. Brian explained what had happened and added that of the two alternatives, he had chosen to resign. Vivienne replied that by doing this he had played into their hands.

It was then that Brian realised how it would look to the loyal Yorkshire supporters who had only recently contributed to his benefit. He had taken their money and walked out on them. Even worse was the thought that he had let the team down by deserting during a period of transition. Most of all, it mattered what might happen to the team. He believed in it and loved it with a tremendous passion and it had been snatched away from him.

Brian began to feel angry and felt that he deserved better than to leave on such a basis. He telephoned Headingley, to tell them that he had changed his mind and decided to face dismissal. Unfortunately, he was informed that the statement concerning his resignation had already been issued; well in advance of the time specified, as it happened. The die was cast.

A number of Yorkshire members formed an action group in an effort to reform the committee and change the way the county was run. Gradually the officials were forced into making short statements and the press wheedled more information from committee members. Eventually a picture began to emerge. Apparently Brian's services were no longer required, for three reasons. He did not develop young players sufficiently, he was not fit and he criticised one-day cricket.

The first two of these accusations, he felt, were unjustified. As for the third, Brian has never made any secret of the fact that he thinks one-day cricket is bad for the game, but so too have many others. He recalls upsetting Brian Sellers, on a previous occasion, with his views on the one-day game. These included the statement that, being expected to act like clowns, they might as well look like them. He was referring to the colourful and conspicuous attire worn by players in one-day matches.

Cartoon

Viv Richards, nurtured by Brian at Somerset CCC.

Nothing came of the members' protests and Brian was given no opportunity to refute the accusations. He was out on a limb and left to swallow the bitter pill of unwarranted rejection.

Following the turmoil of his sacking, it took several months before Brian was able to think rationally again about his career. He still loved the game and wanted to carry on playing. Approaches were made from other counties for his services, which raised his dampened spirits. He took another job outside of sport and was told by the company's chairman that they would like him to carry on playing first-class cricket.

Somerset had been the first county to show an interest in him, but, despite their repeated phone calls, Brian was in no state to follow anything up. As his mind cleared he became interested in joining them and went to meet their officials. He got on well with the people that he met, warming to their attitude and future plans for the county. After discussing the prospects with Vivienne, he decided to join them.

Thus began another phase in Brian's remarkable cricket career. During his first season with Somerset he played happily under the captaincy of Brian Langford and formed a good relationship with their established players. He enjoyed a new lease of life, which was reflected in his performance. That season he topped the batting averages and hit five centuries, a source of immense satisfaction to him.

The following season he was asked to take over the captaincy. He had enjoyed the taste of freedom associated with playing without the responsibility of leadership and did not want to give it up. However, he was persuaded that he could be a great help to the club and especially the younger players, if he took over. Brian relented and found himself back in a position from which he had been forcibly removed for not encouraging young players!

There were early struggles and occasions when the playing staff was sorely tried. At that time Somerset was not a rich county and due to injuries had difficulties fielding eleven players, let alone a balanced side. But the team played good, attractive cricket and began to draw in the crowds. They could not afford to hire established players wanting moves from other counties, so they threw everything into developing young talent. Several youngsters were signed, including a promising batsman from Antigua called

Vivian Richards and the outlook became optimistic.

Following a great deal of hard work and practice things began to develop. Somerset finished fifth in the championship, were semi-finalists in both the Gillette and Benson and Hedges competitions and runners-up to Leicestershire in the John Player League. Viv Richards began to produce glimpses of the great talent that was to come and a young player by the name of Ian Botham was establishing himself as a fine all-rounder

Unfortunately, the outstanding successes of his period as captain of Yorkshire were not repeated, mainly through injuries, particularly those to Somerset's outstanding bowler, Tom Cartwright. Despite these setbacks a useful side was developed and Brian enjoyed leading it. His proudest achievement at the county was his involvement in the development of Viv Richards and Ian Botham, who became legends during their careers.

Another event, of which he is justly proud, compensated somewhat for his county's lack of sustained success. In 1975 he went to Buckingham Palace to receive a CBE. It was an unforgettable day for Brian and his family.

During his time at Somerset Brian was recalled, on several occasions, to the England team. In the early 1970's he was invited to captain the national side in the one-day series against Australia. It felt good to be in charge of England once more, especially as they won the series.

When the West Indies toured over here in 1976 Brian played in the first three matches of the series, acquitting himself well against their battery of bowlers that included Holding, Daniel, Julien and Holder. Despite his accomplishment, in the second Test, of scoring sixty runs in the first innings and forty-six in the second, he was dropped after the batting debacle of the third Test, when England were dismissed for seventy-one in the first innings and fared only marginally better in the second. Several other batsmen, who had hardly covered themselves in glory, kept their places, whilst Brian was left out for the remainder of the series.

The 1977 cricket season began badly for him. Illness and injury kept him out of the team until it was well underway. During his period of absence Brian had time to contemplate and realised that for the past seven years he had spent the best part of six months of each year away from his wife and their two growing children. He also had a nagging shoulder injury that restricted his throwing the ball and felt that he could not get totally involved in all aspects of the game. On top of this, he sensed that, having built a useful team of good young players at Somerset, he was now keeping one of them out of the side.

All these factors contributed to his decision to retire at the end of that season, but it was not made lightly. He had badly wanted to win a trophy for Somerset, the county that had given him such a warm and sincere welcome when his cricket career was on the rocks. Unfortunately, it was not to be, but the disappointment was outweighed by the opportunity to rejoin his family and to become a full-time husband and father.

He was now free to enjoy life with his family and to indulge his many other interests, such as fishing, golf, squash and tennis. Horse-racing has always been a hobby and he is particularly stirred by the racing stride of a well-trained thoroughbred. The opportunities for a day at the races, which he greatly enjoys, became more frequent. He has made many friends within the sport and when he was captain of Yorkshire, he had several outings with his team to Middleham, in Wensleydale, which has a great horse-racing tradition. Here they played friendly cricket matches against teams of jockeys and stable staff, who were allowed to field twenty-two players, to even the odds!

Brian's greatest satisfaction, resulting from twenty-eight years in first-class cricket, is the memory of playing in the distinctive Yorkshire side of the 1960's, which won seven championships and two Gillette Cups. It was a period of great excitement coupled with the thrill of playing with fantastic colleagues.

He holds positive and outspoken views on the modern game, for he possesses one of the shrewdest cricketing brains of this, or any other era. Brian continues to think deeply about, and empathise with, the sport that he holds most dear. In his opinion all the changes that have taken place since he retired have not necessarily been for the better, but I am convinced they have not diminished his regard for the game that has also been his life.

CHAPTER SIX

The Changing Face of South Yorkshire

The southernmost area of Yorkshire has recently been targeted by film-makers, buoyed by the success of *The Full Monty*. They have discovered the latent appeal of a land formerly renowned for much earthier occupations, such as steel production and coal-mining.

South Yorkshire is an infant county, established during the re-organisation of administrative and parliamentary boundaries in 1974, but it represents a significant part of the fabric of the old county of Yorkshire. Its landscape is one of rolling hills studded with gritty towns, a sprawling city and innumerable villages that formerly housed a populace that toiled in claustrophobic factories, steelworks and mines. Before the onset of industrialisation, the majority of its terrain consisted of parkland, acres of rich farmland and the broad estates of established and influential families.

Much of the area bounded by Sheffield and Rotherham, in the south, Barnsley, in the north and Doncaster, in the east, comprises the former industrial heartland of Yorkshire. At its zenith, the clang of steam hammers and the screeching of colliery winding-cables were inescapable. A mantle of smoke from myriad chimneys hung over areas of frenetic activity, which gave rise to their own, and the nation's, prosperity and influence.

Rasping hooters, that called workers to their daily stint, are all but silenced and pit-head winding-gear has vanished from the landscape like springtime snow. Gone are the mountainous spoil heaps that loomed over regimented rows of colliery houses, threatening to engulf entire communities as they became increasingly distended. Much of the coalfield is returning to its natural state. Open cast workings and foreboding slag-heaps have been landscaped and great tracts of scarred terrain are once more blending with the green carpet that surrounds them. The massive steelworks of Sheffield and Rotherham have, of necessity, been scaled down and the pall of smoke that engulfed them has drifted into the mists of time.

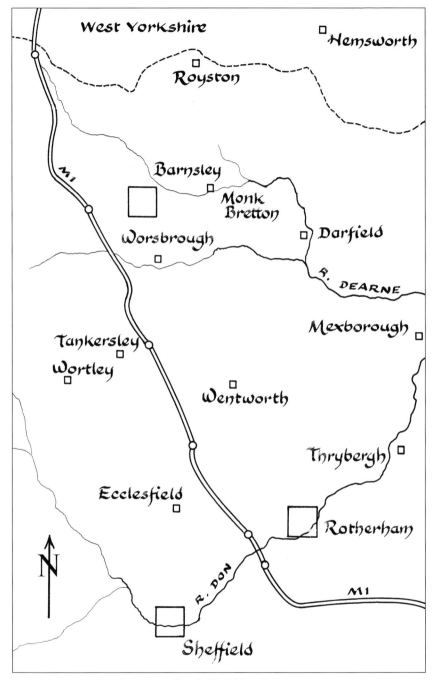

South Yorkshire-1

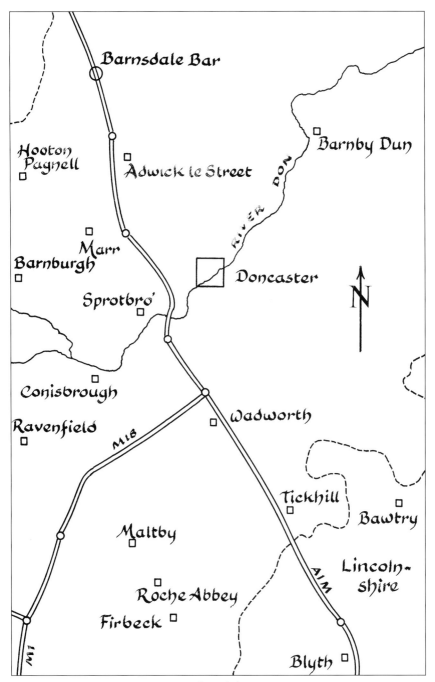

South Yorkshire-2

Today, South Yorkshire is bedecked with country parks, lakes, scenic reservoirs and nature reserves. Footpaths and bridleways abound and the county is about to be traversed by a purpose-built walkway and cycle route that is currently under construction. This coast to coast route, the Trans Pennine Trail, is a Millennium project intended for walkers, cyclists, horseriders and, wherever possible, for people using wheelchairs and pushchairs. It is due for completion at the end of the year 2000 but many sections are already available for use. The Trail will run from Southport to Hornsea and it will eventually form part of a designated European Long Distance Walking Route, the E8, which goes all the way to Istanbul.

The attractive stretch of countryside bounded by the towns of Barnsley, Doncaster and Rotherham is covered in this chapter. Today it is rich in rural attractions, including the principal rivers that drain it, the Dearne and the Don.

The River Dearne winds through Barnsley, a progressive town, dubbed 'Black Barnsley' by Daniel Defoe, which is a shining example of the regeneration of the county's grimy industrial past. In the nineteenth century it developed from a small rural township into the hub of one of Britain's major coalfields and probably lived up to Defoe's description. Things have changed dramatically in recent decades, however, with the advent of considerable re-development.

Barnsley's rebirth is not confined to its buildings. Several local organisations have in recent years been actively involved in its environmental and economic improvement. The Barnsley Development Agency embraces an Economic Regeneration Team that is actively encouraging local investment and the establishment of new businesses in the area.

The original staple industries of the locality, mining and glass manufacture are a thing of the past, although the latter is still produced on a much smaller scale. Some manufacturing still survives and the creation of business and commercial sites is being pursued. Employment is being stimulated by new ventures in communications and the utilisation of Barnsley's favourable geographical situation, for logistics purposes. It is ideally placed in relation to road and motorway infrastructure and the installation of distribution depots is the ultimate aim.

The Dearne is no longer choked with the contamination

Cusworth Hall near Doncaster

Firbeck

Firsby Hall Farm

All Saints Square, Rotherham

prevalent during the industrial era as it skirts the bustling town centre, with its modern shopping precincts and flourishing market. There have been markets in the town since 1249 and the current one is amongst the largest in the north. It is justly proud of its traditional fare, such as national and international award-winning Yorkshire puddings and pies.

Barnsley's lattice-work of busy streets is hemmed with colonnades of tidy stone and brick facades that remain largely unnoticed by the multitudes that throng the array of shops beneath. Set amongst this hub of activity, in Peel Square, is a reminder of the locality's mining heritage, in the form of two refurbished mining cars that formerly carried up to two tons of coal from the workings to the surface.

An imposing Town Hall presides over the busy township. Perched on a prominent hill, this distinctive landmark was opened by the future King Edward VIII in 1933. Its eye-catching tower compliments the nearby fifteenth-century one belonging to the Parish Church of St. Mary the Virgin. The only detraction from the view presented by the elevated crest of the town is the undistinguished 1960's-style concrete carbuncle that is a constituent of Barnsley College.

Modern buildings such as this pale into insignificance alongside older and more decorative structures like the one occupied by the National Union of Mineworkers. Built in the 1870's, it is the former headquarters of the Yorkshire Mineworkers' Association and it became known as 'King Arthur's Castle,' after its most combative incumbent, Arthur Scargill.

To counteract its urbanisation Barnsley is well served by parks and recreation areas. Within a mile of the town centre lies Locke Park, which extends for nearly fifty acres. It was created as a memorial to Joseph Locke, one of the district's important figures in the nineteenth century. Educated at Barnsley Grammar School, he became apprenticed to George Stephenson and blossomed into a significant railway builder in his own right. His wife donated the park to the town in 1861 and a bronze statue of her husband stands within it.

As it casts off Barnsley's urban confines, the Dearne flows between tree-lined banks speckled with the varied hues of laburnum, hollyhocks and wild camomile. It soon reaches another splendid recreational site on the outskirts of the town, Dearne Valley Park, which was conceived in 1980 by the local authority and financed under its Urban Reclamation Scheme. Now that the river's quality has been greatly improved it is a pleasant pastime to follow its progress through the park and look for the assortment of fish that it once again supports. There is, in fact, no shortage of fish in the park, for it also contains an attractive lake, which is stocked with carp, perch, tench and bream. Anyone may fish in the lake, free of charge.

Within the park is a nature reserve, containing a mixed plantation that provides a suitable habitat for small birds, rodents and bank voles. This is complimented by oak and birch woods that cloak much of the valley within which the park lies.

In addition to a children's play area, a cycleway traverses the park, which connects the town centre with the Dorothy Hyman Sports Centre at nearby Cudworth and also links into the Trans Pennine Trail that utilises a disused local railway network as it passes through the locality. The Barnsley area lies at the heart of the project, for this is where offshoot sections of the Trail, from Leeds and Chesterfield, will merge with the coast to coast route.

Two landmarks overlook the park, which provide Barnsley with its distinctive character. The first is the football stadium at Oakwell, a mecca for local soccer enthusiasts, which exhibits a modern façade of metal girders and concrete that dominates the skyline. The homely club has had a brief flirtation with the Premier League in recent times, but unfortunately it did not possess the resources to ensure success in football's top flight.

Hidden amongst trees that thickly coat an adjoining hillside stands the second feature; the silent and forlorn winding-gear of the disused Barnsley Main Colliery. This relic of Barnsley's industrial past, along with the surrounding land, has been in the care of the local authority since 1992. They have landscaped the site and are preserving it for future generations. It presents a sober reminder of the harshness and danger that was the miner's lot.

One of the worst tragedies to befall the local mining community occurred in the mid-eighteen-hundreds when an underground explosion claimed the lives of 361 men and boys. Many perished through horrific burns when their fate was sealed by the build up of volatile fire-damp gases due to poor ventilation. The colliery owners

A South Yorkshire Miner

had considered improved aeration to be too expensive.

The Barnsley Canal formerly accompanied the River Dearne as it leaves the town and meanders through the Dearne Valley. Many sections of this derelict waterway have disappeared, but during its heyday it was a vital trading artery that, in the early nineteenth century, gave rise to a number of collieries, which were established along its route. All these have been abandoned but it is possible to detect where the loading basins were located in some of the wider sections that have been dug out and restored. Restoration work is currently being carried out on the canal, under the auspices of the Barnsley Trades Council, to provide work experience for the unemployed.

Barges transported coal from the locality along the canal and onwards to places such as York and Ripon. They would call at Knottingley on their return journey, to pick up limestone that was used for local land improvement.

A few miles south-east of Barnsley the canal joins the Dove and Dearne Canal, which was built as an alternative route for the export of Barnsley coal to Hull, by linking up with the Don Navigation. Many other loads were carried along the canal network, such as iron from the foundries in and around Barnsley, millstones from Wharncliffe and oak bark bound for the leather tanneries.

The River Dearne continues south-east from Dearne Valley Park on a scenic journey to its junction with the River Don, on the outskirts of Conisbrough. Its companion is the Dearne Way, a combination of paths and bridleways that accompany the unfettered river through the lush Dearne Valley, which encompasses some of South Yorkshire's finest countryside

A little of Barnsley's early history is revealed, as river and path pass the remains of Monk Bretton Priory. The monastery was founded in 1153 for monks of the Cluniac order, but by 1281 it had changed to the Benedictine order. At the Dissolution, the buildings were significantly stripped and the north aisle of the nave was removed and rebuilt at Wentworth Church. Its remains are extensive, but mainly ruinous. Apart from the Prior's lodging and the south wall of the refectory, little remains but the foundations and lower courses. One outstanding feature, a main drain, can be discerned, which represents a tribute to monastic sanitation.

The abbey's history is punctuated with bitter strife and legal disputes involving the local people, its nearby mother Priory at Pontefract and consequently, Rome. These altercations were caused by the monks claiming complete jurisdiction over properties and riches, which they had amassed. Anger flared when Pontefract sent an unpopular monk to become the Prior of Monk Bretton, causing the monks to despatch a deputation to the mother abbey at Cluny, in France. The representatives from Yorkshire, instead of receiving a sympathetic hearing, were imprisoned and abused. Another deputation was sent to Rome and was more successful, regaining their power to elect a Prior without interference. However, it was ruled that the Prior of Pontefract should conduct his installation and that token payments would be made to Pontefract in place of the higher sums being demanded.

A short distance past the Priory, the river is crossed by the first of a series of dismantled railways that it encounters. These provide another example of industrial demise. A network of tracks, principally transporting coal, linked many of the mining sites to steelworks and factories. Along the bed of these former railways run footpaths and bridleways, which provide excellent walking conditions.

The river meanders towards Darfield through an agricultural landscape that until recently was dominated by enormous expanses of arable crops. The Environment Committee of the South Yorkshire County Council and the Countryside Commission are actively pursuing schemes to improve its appearance and increase opportunities for wildlife.

One example is underway at the joint farm holding of Tyers Hall and Tyers Hill that extends over 350 acres. During recent years the present owners have built up a herd of Jersey cows and several miles of hedgerows have been planted to provide stock-proof barriers. A large part of the land is now mixed arable and ley pasture, interspersed with recently planted trees. Existing woodland is being managed, to benefit wildlife.

A long history of farming exists at Tyers Hall and Tyers Hill, whose farmhouses and outbuildings date back to the seventeenth and eighteenth centuries. Aerial reconnaissance has revealed field boundaries and ditches laid down around 2000 years ago by the

A South Yorkshire Colliery

Romans. During this period Darfield was an important settlement, for collections of gold coins have been unearthed and a Roman road is known to have passed through the district.

As Darfield is approached, the prominent tower of its fifteenth-century church beckons from a garland of trees. The lower portion of the tower dates from the twelfth century and built into the stonework are the remains of an earlier church, constructed in the eighth century. Within its precincts resides a royal coat of arms, cast in plaster, belonging to Elizabeth I that was discovered in a local sixteenth-century farmhouse, now demolished.

The accompanying graveyard contains a column marking the last resting-place of ten miners who plunged to their deaths in a cage-winding accident on New Year's Eve 1886. Also in the churchyard lies the tomb of Ebenezer Elliot, known as the 'Corn Law Rhymer,' who was a poet and social reformer. He was an ardent campaigner for the abolition of the Corn Law, before his death in 1849.

Darfield, its name probably derived from 'Deer-field,' expanded rapidly in the mid-nineteenth century when mine- shafts were sunk in the locality.

Cutting the bottom layers of coal

As it passes through the village, the river is crossed by Darfield Bridge, which formerly carried a turnpike road, constructed in 1740. Near the bridge stands the old whitewashed Toll Bar House, built to extract payment from travellers for the upkeep of the road, which still retains the name, Saltergate Road. Salt was transported in carts from Cheshire to the market towns of South Yorkshire along this important trans-Pennine route. The vital commodity was much in demand in those times, for large quantities were used to preserve meat following the annual slaughter of livestock.

Three miles beyond Darfield the Dearne skirts another ancient village, Bolton on Dearne that retains the feel of an Anglo-Saxon settlement, which existed during the ninth century. At that time the local St Andrews Church was built and traces of the original building can still be detected.

The nearby village of Harlington is linked to the riverside by a dismantled railway that forms part of the Dearne Way. This broad highway, elevated on a grassy embankment, provides excellent views along a tranquil section of the river, which it follows for approximately two miles. Sheltering rushes and reeds intrude into its dark waters, creating a good breeding habitat that may eventually provide a home for rarer species of bird, such as bittern, and marsh harrier.

Riverside fields display splashes of vivid-yellow, where oil seed rape has encroached into surrounding cereal crops. Stately poplars thrust between the houses of Harlington, which, along with its neighbour, Barnburgh, lies in a landscape patterned by luxurious hedgerows and trees. The architects of this rewarding outlook were the great estate owners, the Montagues, who ensured that the pits they owned were well hidden from their nearby residence at Melton Hall. Thus Harlington and Barnburgh have remained largely unaltered over the passing years, whilst on the opposite side of the river industrial communities have spawned around Mexborough.

One of the Montagues' collieries was tucked away on the outskirts of Barnburgh, but all that remains today is a solitary winding-wheel, erected at the roadside near the pit's former entrance and bearing the inscription 'Barnburgh Colliery 1913-1989'.

A pivotal point of Barnburgh, the attractive St Peters Church, has an impressive tower that is clearly visible from the river and it presides over the scene of a remarkable tale. Sir Percival Cresacre, a Knight Templar in the fifteenth century, was, according to tradition, attacked by a wild cat whilst returning home one night by horse from Doncaster. The ensuing battle reputedly lasted several hours before both combatants died in the doorway of the church. An oak figure of Sir Percival, the local lord of the manor, can be found in the church and the carving of a cat is exhibited on the church tower, in addition to being incorporated into the Cresacre family crest.

Beyond Barnburgh, in earlier times, lay the ancient forest of Barnsdale, where Robin Hood reputedly spent much of his time. This great tract of woodland, between Doncaster and Pontefract, has virtually disappeared, but its name survives to this day, through the junction on the A1 trunk road, called Barnsdale Bar. Not far from the busy intersection lies Robin Hood's Well, so called since the reign of Henry VII, which has a stone canopy above it designed by Vanburgh.

At Denaby Ings, situated a little farther down the River Dearne, mining subsidence has helped to create a large stretch of open water, as it has in several other parts of the surrounding area. These bands of water are now managed as nature reserves by the Yorkshire Wildlife Trust, with support from South Yorkshire County Council. Denaby Ings presents a restful mosaic of unruffled water, reed swamp and hay-meadows, an ideal habitat for wildfowl that includes teal, mallard, great-crested grebe, tufted duck and moorhen. Convenient hides are provided from which to observe the wildlife and centre-stage is regularly occupied by three cormorants that perch on the stark branches of a dead tree marooned on an island within the lake.

It is a short walk from Denaby Ings to the confluence of the rivers Dearne and Don along a scenic path that is unfortunately hemmed by waste-high foliage that includes nettles and briars. One consolation for wading through the stinging undergrowth is the view of the keep of Conisbrough Castle that lies across the river, amidst a verdant backdrop.

Before joining the more expansive River Don on its journey to Doncaster, it is worthwhile to follow the Dearne Way into the adjacent industrial town of Mexborough. It stands alongside the Don that is a navigable from Sheffield until it joins the Dutch canal that links it to the Humber at Goole. This section of the Don forms the Sheffield and South Yorkshire Navigation,

From the mid-eighteenth century until the coming of the railways the waterway carried industrial commodities from the Sheffield region to the port of Hull, for onward shipment to ports around the world. Currently, it is used by pleasure craft and there are regular trips available, by water-bus, from Mexborough to Doncaster.

Mexborough has its share of history, both ancient and recent. In a small wooded park on its outskirts lie the remains of Mexborough Castle, built by the Norman conquerors to guard a strategic ford across the River Don. The existing mounds cover the site of an even older fortress dating back to the famous Battle of Maisbelly in 488, where the Britons fought and slew the Saxon warrior Hengist.

Around Mexborough, in the latter half of the nineteenth century, shafts were sunk at Denaby, Manvers Main and Cadeby. There were two kinds of pit at that time; those owned by the landed gentry, such as the 'Fitzbillys,' as the Earls of Fitzwilliam were known and those of the wealthy entrepreneurs.

Disputes were rare at the Manvers family pit, but at Denaby and Cadeby strikes and lock-outs were common. The colliers gained a reputation for dogged militancy, whilst the owners were renowned for being amongst the most uncompromising in the West Riding.

Tension spilled over in 1902 when the great 'bag-muck' strike broke out. The miners wanted payment for removing thick layers of bag-dirt, which separates the layers of coal. In the winter of 1903, with the strike in its seventh month, the employers evicted 720 families from the company-owned cottages in Denaby. After severe hardship the strike ended in defeat for the beleaguered colliers when the courts ordered the cessation of strike pay by the Yorkshire Mineworkers' Association.

One of the most attractive suburbs of Mexborough is the hamlet of Old Denaby that has retained a quiet charm, despite its proximity to Denaby Main, the scene of some of the worst mining disturbances. This collection of desirable residences, with their gardens bathed in colour, lends an air of serenity and accomplishment to the locality.

An added appeal of Old Denaby is its proximity to a rewarding lake, with surrounding marshland, which supports a variety of bird-life and a plentiful supply of fish.

On the outskirts of Conisbrough, near the meeting of the Dearne and the Don, the Trans Pennine Trail can be joined, for a gratifying three-mile journey to the historic village of Sprotbrough. Close by stands the Earth Centre, occupying the former site of Cadeby Colliery, which closed in 1986, with devastating effects on the local community.

In 1995 the Millenium Commission allocated fifty million pounds for the creation of this ultra-modern complex that is dedicated to the protection of the environment. The surrounding land is being regenerated to enhance and protect important habitats and 60,000 trees have already been planted.

The ethos of this Millenium project is to raise people's environmental awareness and to promote the preservation of our planet. Ecological and forward thinking is the hallmark of the unique Centre, which comprises exciting, innovative buildings and surroundings that utilise interactive features and exhibitions for the public, particularly children, to enjoy.

From the Earth Centre the Trail takes a high-level course

through the preservation area, which has been allowed to revert to its natural state. One passes through a vibrant array of wild flowers, such as monk's hood, camomile and rose-bay willow herb, that flourish amongst a waving carpet of grass. Fledgling trees also sprout from this natural wilderness.

The beckoning keep of Conisbrough Castle looms large across the Don. Occupying a strategic and appealing position above the town, the prominent edifice was revered by Sir Walter Scott, who featured it in his novel, *Ivanhoe.*

It is likely that Conisbrough was a bergh of the ninth-century Northumbrian kings and it is dominated by two hills, one bearing the church and the other the castle. An early version of the castle, probably nothing more than a defensive earthwork, was the property of King Harold. It was converted into one of the finest medieval fortresses in England by Hamelin Plantaganet, the half brother of Henry II, to whom the estate passed in 1163. It represented a potent symbol of feudal strength and power and even today the ruins of its strong limestone ramparts evoke the splendour and brutality of that bygone age.

Dominating the site is the ninety feet tall circular keep, which has been recently renovated. The walls of this impressive structure are supported by substantial buttresses, which provide an unusual spectacle. Within the keep the design is ingenious, for the hall is on the first floor and above it are the solar and chapel.

Despite its apparent impregnability, fortresses such as this sometimes fell victim to subterfuge. This offered a subtle alternative to a straightforward siege, which could be long and expensive, with no guarantee of success. One method involved a small group of men seeking to infiltrate the castle and then open the gates to the main attacking force. For such a venture, a stinking latrine chute at the base of the walls might provide an opportunity for courageous individuals with a strong constitution. At least one seemingly impregnable fortification was taken by this ploy. Under cover of darkness a small group of trusted men helped a comrade make undetected entry to the keep through an unbarred latrine opening, high up its wall.

Other ruses included attackers, disguised as tradesmen, entering a castle on market day, when local townspeople were allowed in. Their baskets would contain weapons instead of produce and once

A bus of 1934 vintage

inside they could overpower the sentries and attempt to capture the fortress.

As it leaves the preservation area the Trail descends to the Don, where it passes a soaring viaduct and burrows through protective banks of great willow herb, poppy and knapweed that provide a riot of colour in the early summer. Birdsong accompanies your footsteps along the riverside and a nature reserve, Sprotbrough Flash, is entered, where archways of ash, maple and rowan provide cool shade. Nearby lies an extensive mere, which is a magnet for nesting birds.

Evidence of the cleanliness of the River Don is provided by the multitude of fishermen that line its banks, particularly on Sundays when fiercely contested competitions are held. Fishing tackle abounds and tubular, padded seats provide comfort. They are placed in shallow water to provide convenient access to fish lurking in the depths. Attached to these seats are a variety of trays for holding bait, twine, implements and food.

The Don skirts Sprotbrough, but it is only a short walk into the centre of the village, by a route which passes the Old Rectory. Two intriguing fixtures can be found outside this mature building, one

Conisbrough Castle

standing near the main entrance, the other mounted on the wall adjacent to a side gate. The first of these, is the village pump. A remnant of a bygone age, it shelters within a weathered-stone surround that bears an ancient crest.

The second is a plaque, which indicates that Sir Douglas Bader, the famous legless wartime fighter pilot, lived here during his boyhood, in the early 1920's.

Sprotbrough was the original home of the Fitzwilliam family. In the Middle Ages it was important enough to have a regular market and the base of the ancient market cross can be seen near the entrance to the churchyard. In those early times, the settlement was a refuge for criminals, as well as for the hungry. Wrongdoers could claim sanctuary in the church by sitting in the sanctuary chair, which is still to be found there. Fugitives who managed to reach the chair were spared immediate retribution by their pursuers, but were still liable to a judicial trial and banishment if found guilty.

The Church of St Mary, Sprotbrough, is an historical treasure-house, whose beginnings can be traced back to the twelfth century. A time-worn stone pillar, standing near the present pulpit, has provided a means of support since around 1180 and the fabric of the building remains much as it was at the time of the Reformation, 450 years ago.

Many interesting features can be found within, for in addition to the unique fourteenth-century sanctuary chair, it houses elaborately carved pew ends, a delicately-fashioned medieval Chancel Screen, funeral shields, and a clock-face, with a dummy hand, mounted above the organ.

The existing pews, installed in 1915, replace the old box pews, whose doors are retained as pew ends. The carvings on these doors include a pair of figures skittishly illustrating 'before and after marriage,' one being carved with two heads facing each other and another with heads back to back.

Its original drive now inoperable, the ornamental clock-face provides an unusual adornment that can perplex visitors to the church. It commemorates Gertrude Copley, who died in 1710. She was a member of a notable local family, joined by marriage to the Fitzwilliams.

The age of the Chancel Screen has been the subject of much conjecture, but it was probably the work of a local craftsman in the early sixteenth century.

Several colourful funeral shields, or hatchments, adorn the walls and bear the coat of arms of noteworthy deceased persons. Such shields were originally hung outside the door of the house where they died before being placed in the church.

Sprotbrough, like its neighbour, Conisbrough, has connections with Sir Walter Scott, who stayed there whilst obtaining material for *Ivanhoe*. The Ivanhoe Hotel, which stands on the outskirts of the village, provides a salient reference to this historic novel

Sprotbrough Lock has to be negotiated before further progress can be made along the Don towards Doncaster. Prior to the lock stands a welcome inn, adjacent to a popular landing-stage, which is a stopping point for the water-bus.

The Trail continues to follow the river as it winds towards Doncaster and passes under the A1(M) that is mounted on tall concrete stilts. In the vicinity of two imposing, but unfortunately redundant, railway viaducts, the Trans Pennine Trail ceases its riverside journey.

A pleasant waterside path, however, is available from this point that provides agreeable views of surrounding meadows, flecked with copses, as it rides on a grassy embankment for much of the journey into Doncaster.

The only drawback to this rural idyll is the disquieting notices, erected on several stiles, warning people to beware of bulls, cows and calves.

As it approaches the town, a bleaker landscape of warehouses, factories and high-rise flats unfolds. This is tempered by the appearance of several modern and aesthetic brick-built premises that sprout from the urban canvas.

Doncaster is another settlement that is steeped in history. From around 70 A.D. a Roman fort, known as Danum, stood there, on the line of the Roman road, Watling Street. Many relics from this period have been unearthed and are on display in a local museum.

In Saxon times, the village, as it was then, was named Dona Ceaster and it later developed into a township, primarily due to transport. In the eighteenth century Doncaster was an important coaching halt on the Great North Road, which is now the A1 trunk road. A century later it was a strategic canal centre and eventually became a hub of the railway network in the north, due to its position on the main line to London.

As a result of the rapid growth of the railways, the Great Northern Railway workshops were moved there in 1853 and the town continued to expand. The famous *Flying Scotsman* was built in the workshops and made railroad history in 1934 by being the first locomotive to reach the speed of 100 m.p.h. This outstanding product of the steam age made a recent welcome return to its birthplace, stopping off en route to York on a celebratory journey, following a multi-million pound refit. Hundreds of railway enthusiasts and onlookers packed the station, eagerly seizing the opportunity to photograph this fine example of railway history.

Doncaster also achieved recognition as a farmer's market town and has maintained this role for the region, with full markets held every week, selling a wide variety of merchandise. It continues to be a focal point for a populace that has experienced the decline of the mining industry. In order to counteract this deterioration, the local authority is providing a greater focus on the rural aspects of the borough, coupled with encouragement for new business and commercial opportunities.

The sport of horse-racing has been vibrantly connected with the town for centuries. It boasts the oldest classic horserace, named after Colonel, later General, Anthony St Leger, who lived in the area more than 200 years ago. A keen racegoer, he initiated a sweepstake of twenty-five guineas each for three-year-olds, to be run over two miles at Doncaster in 1776.

Purists may argue that the race was actually begun two years later, when a function took place at the local Red Lion Inn. The gathering of horse-racing personalities was indeed the first occasion that the event received its familiar name. But for the generosity of the Marquis of Rockingham it would have been called the 'Rockingham Stakes.' He modestly declined to sanction this title, stating that the idea for such a race belonged to Colonel St Leger.

This annual classic race, run in September, attracts a worldwide following and it has brought great influence and prestige to the town. Local hotels and guest-houses are heavily in demand, not only at this time, but whenever race meetings are taking place.

The Mansion House, designed by James Paine and completed in 1748, was the setting for many banquets and balls during the St Leger meetings and its splendid façade still overlooks High Street. It remains one of only three civic mansion houses in England and continues to be a centre for civic business and social activity, a role for which it was originally intended. This jewel in Doncaster's crown draws admiring glances from all who encounter it, particularly at night, when its exquisite Georgian lines bask under the spell of discreet floodlights.

An able companion to this bastion of civic pride is nearby Clock Corner, where a distinguished timepiece gazes down on the junction of French Gate and Baxter Gate. This gives a further historical aspect to the town and it provides a symbol of continuity amidst the surrounding labyrinth of pedestrianised precincts and modern shopping centres.

Doncaster was formerly at the centre of the largest coalfield in the country. Although it is still reliant on industry, the importance of the increased opportunities for leisure is fully appreciated and has resulted in the provision of a multi-million pound complex opposite the racecourse that caters for a multitude of sports and contains a multi-screen cinema and bowling alley. A marina and other facilities are currently under construction.

Featuring highly amongst other local attractions is Cusworth Hall, situated in a prominent position amidst acres of surrounding parkland, on the outskirts of the town. The estate was purchased by the Wrightson family in 1669. They created a village within it, which included agricultural buildings and worker's cottages, during the next century. In the 1740's, the present hall was built and it provides a stirring backdrop to the lakeland landscape of what is now a country park. The estate is currently owned by Doncaster Metropolitan Borough and admission to the hall and grounds is free. A Museum of South Yorkshire Life occupies the hall and depicts life in the locality over the last 200 years.

At the rear of the hall, well-manicured lawns roll down to a reed-lined lake, inhabited by coot, moorhen and a variety of fish. Surrounding woodland, dappled with tranquil pools, provides a natural habitat for birds and reclusive animals. Also, a network of paths radiates around the congenial parkland, which is bounded by extensive fields of swaying wheat and barley.

Cusworth Hall is easily distinguishable from the nearby A1(M) and from its elevated site, the slender, decorous tower of Doncaster Parish Church can be clearly seen.

The elegant Parish Church of St George is an outstanding example of Victorian neo-Gothic architecture and its elaborate stonework exhibits an array of intricate carvings. Within the church is a nationally renowned organ, which, at the time of its installation in 1862, was the largest in the country. It was designed and built by Edmund Schulze, who was invited to the Great Exhibition of 1851 by Prince Albert. His expertise was widely admired and the prince, who was impressed by his skill, asked him to provide an organ for an English church.

Amongst the list of leading organists that have played at the church was the notable composer, Edward Miller, who lived in the area during the eighteenth century and unfortunately would not have had the opportunity to perform on the Schulze organ. His most widely known composition is the tune 'Rockingham,' for the hymn *When I Survey the Wondrous Cross.*

There are many more attractions to the featured area of South Yorkshire. The pleasant rolling countryside to the south of Doncaster and the east of Rotherham is studded with historic sites, such as Roche Abbey. Inviting villages like Firbeck and

The Mansion House, Doncaster

Ravenfield are common and it harbours its share of rural retreats. These attributes provide a pleasant contrast to the dour, industrial villages that formerly characterised the region.

Roche Abbey, whose remnants stand near Maltby, was named after an unusual rock formation, which resembled a cross and was a place of pilgrimage. Built of local stone, this Cistercian outpost has stood in the valley of the River Ryton since the twelfth century. Flanked by limestone cliffs and surrounded by sheltered meadows, carpeted with daffodils in spring, the twin towers of its crumbling gatehouse rise above a landscape that was created by Capability Brown. The Abbey fell into decay after the Dissolution, but many attractive features remain to indicate its former splendour.

Within two miles of this eminent site stands notable Sandbeck Hall, formerly one of the finest residences in the country. This is the former home of the Lumleys, or, to give them their proper title, the Earls of Scarborough. The family has a long and colourful history. One earl fought courageously at Flodden, although he had hardly

Roche Abbey

reached manhood.

The hall stands amidst spacious Sandbeck Park and it was one of the earls who commissioned Capability Brown to landscape some of the grounds and the adjacent site of Roche Abbey.

Nearby Firbeck is the tidiest of villages whose main street is lined with neat stone walls behind which hide trim, pantile-roofed cottages. Symmetrically fashioned bushes protrude above the walls to shield windows from the gaze of passers-by. A dignified and well-established stone house also overlooks the main thoroughfare, its façade enhanced by mullioned windows and a thick tangle of pendulous wisteria that coats its gable end. It provides a decorative backdrop to a row of roadside tubs containing clusters of multi-coloured flowers and cascading palms.

One almost tiptoes through this pristine settlement, nestling in the Ryton Valley, anxious not to disturb its serenity. The red-roofed cottages and mellow stone walls are reminiscent of the communities that huddle in the folds of the North York Moors.

The area to the east of Rotherham is a peaceful rural haven. Conisbrough Parks comprises an expanse of mature meadows and rolling acres of arable land. Footpaths scythe through boundless fields of long-stemmed corn and butterflies flutter around hedgerows that border the quiet country lanes, which criss-cross the agricultural landscape.

A series of reservoirs speckle the countryside around Ravenfield and Thrybergh. At Firsby a cluster of small water sources can be found, which resemble scenic lakes rather than reservoirs and these, along with nearby Thrybergh Reservoir, were constructed during the 1870's to provide drinking water for Doncaster. Garlands of wild flowers and rushes surround them and in the spring, adjacent meadows and hawthorn copses are carpeted with bluebells. This idyll, known as the Firsby Reservoirs Nature Reserve, is a habitat for grey heron, red bunting, great spotted woodpecker, kestrel and skylark. These inhabitants have discovered the valuable marsh and willow carr that has developed through the silting up of the reservoirs, which are also home to mallard, blue damselfly and three-spined stickleback.

Within Ravenfield Park, a string of ponds has been developed as an angling facility and concessionary footpaths provide access to those wishing to explore the area. The ponds are home to several species of plant, including yellow water-lily and the surrounding wooded slopes echo with the screeching of jays. In winter, the cones of birch and alder provide welcome food for redpoll and siskin.

Tall banks of dazzling oil seed rape coat the fields that skirt Ravenfield, a picturesque hamlet with an exceedingly attractive church. Its shapely tower, crowned with a steeple, can be seen rising from a protective fringe of woodland that lines the edge of Ravenfield Park.

Thrybergh Reservoir provides an equally rewarding spectacle. Much larger than those at Firsby, it lies in flat, park-like countryside and offers very pleasant walking around its perimeter, in addition to excellent fishing, windsurfing, canoeing and surfboarding. It forms part of Thrybergh Country Park that houses a visitor centre, car park and a camping and caravan site.

Our final destination is Rotherham, a town that forms a fitting climax to this South Yorkshire journey, for it has done much to dispel its former reputation as a grimy industrial centre.

It was claimed that the pall of smoke over Sheffield and Rotherham was so dense at the outbreak of the Second World War that enemy bombers would never locate their targets. What a contrast now prevails. Although Rotherham is still synonymous with iron and steel production, the dirt and smoke has gone and it is now a garden town set in the heart of a busy industrial region. In recent years it has been consistently successful in the 'Britain in Bloom' competition and was an outright winner of the national title in 1993.

Visitors to the area are surprised to discover that three-quarters of the borough is rural, with rich farmland and extensive woodland. The town centre has a clean, spacious feel and most of its buildings are easy on the eye. Like many towns, it does not completely escape the blight of the construction methods of the 1960's and 1970's. In fact, the view of the graceful Hastings Clock in Effingham Square is somewhat marred by the backdrop of the Civic Building, an unflattering concrete mass that compares unfavourably with the delightful Old Town Hall, which has been imaginatively converted into an extremely tasteful shopping arcade. Within the arcade is the former Mayor's Parlour that has been transformed into a café.

The core of the town centre has been pedestrianised and one can follow broad avenues between tempting rows of shops to the focal point of All Saints Square, which is dominated by the lofty Parish Church and a series of gleaming stainless steel fountains.

Two of Rotherham's historical landmarks stand alongside the modern bridge that spans the River Don. They comprise the remains of the medieval Rotherham Bridge and the ancient, but intact, Chapel on the Bridge that is attached to it. The Chapel of Our Lady, as it is known, was built in 1483, but closed under King Edward VI in 1547. It was rededicated in 1924 and is currently open for worship each Tuesday morning. The old bridge was once the main approach to the town from the north and during the Civil War it was the scene of a valiant, but unsuccessful, defence of Rotherham against the Royalist army of the Earl of Newcastle.

Like its neighbours, Barnsley and Doncaster, Rotherham has undergone a recent period of regeneration, during which the pattern of industry has changed. Most of the local coalmines have closed and despite major manpower reductions, multi-million pound investment in steel production has made it amongst the most profitable in the world. British Steel have an extensive plant on the outskirts of the town and there is a noticeable absence of smoke and fumes emitting from it.

Glass-making, engineering and brass founding are traditional industries that continue to prosper and many new industries have been attracted to the area, such as clothing manufacture, plastics, electronics and food production.

Excellent communications make the town easily accessible. The M1 and M18 motorways traverse the borough and there is good access to all parts of the country by rail. In recent years the Sheffield and South Yorkshire Navigation, which passes through the town centre, has been greatly improved and is increasingly used by both commercial and leisure craft.

CHAPTER SEVEN

The Moors Are My Mistress

In common with Brian Close, a popular song possesses great significance for the celebrated Yorkshire artist, Ashley Jackson. *The Harry Lime Theme* is emblazoned upon his memory, for it forms an accompaniment to a scene, which, in Ashley's words he will 'go out with.'

Strains of the theme tune to the film *The Third Man* drifted across the English Channel from a passing pleasure cruiser as Ashley, an apprehensive and rootless boy of ten, approached our shores on the SS *Canton*. The green slopes of the English coast slowly appeared through a swirling summer mist, seemingly reluctant to reveal themselves to an anxious young onlooker who was about to take his first step onto English soil.

Ashley was en route from Malaya, the country of his birth, with his mother and stepfather, to begin a new chapter in his already eventful life. He had suffered more upheaval in his short lifetime than most of us will ever experience

His birthplace is Penang. Here he entered the troubled arena of south-east Asia, in the local American hospital. The year was 1940 and the spectre of invasion by the Japanese loomed large. His parents, Norman Valentine Jackson, General Manager of the Tiger Beer Company and his teenage wife Dulcie Olga Scott, daughter of a Scottish army band leader, ensured that Ashley's life began with gentility and gracious living. Unfortunately, this was short-lived.

His father enlisted in the local Volunteer Reserve and had the dubious distinction of leading the British contingent during its daunting retreat through the jungles of the Malayan Peninsular to Singapore in 1941. Ashley and his mother moved to that threatened city where his father had set up home for them. During the succeeding months, as life continued with breezy normality, his father, fearing imminent invasion, made plans to ship out the members of his family in separate groups, each to a different country.

This proved a wise move, for at the time of their departure the Japanese army penetrated the seemingly protective jungle and

Ashley Jackson

entered Singapore without serious resistance. Ashley and his mother only just managed to make their escape, with bullets flying and bombs falling as their ship steamed from the harbour. The Japanese had mounted a savage attack on the flotilla of fleeing ships and surrounding vessels were being sunk, much to the distress of his mother who had close friends on several of them

His father stayed behind to fight, as did the men of the family, but to everyone's amazement there was very little conflict, for all regular and irregular forces were ordered to surrender to avoid bloodshed.

Whilst his father was being incarcerated in Changi Prison, Ashley and his mother were evacuated to India. Attempting escape, his father was caught and transferred to a special camp, an oriental version of Colditz, in Borneo. He remained there until the war was entering its final phase. As the advancing Australian troops were about to liberate the camp, his father was given a shovel, ordered to dig his own grave, and then shot.

The memory of this ghastly execution left its mark on the young Ashley, who will never come to terms with the atrocities perpetrated by the Japanese and openly admires the Jews for their perseverance in demanding atonement for those hideous crimes. He is proud to be a patron, in company with Vera Lynn and Harry Secombe, of the Bridge over the River Kwai Association, which is dedicated to helping former soldiers who worked on the infamous Burma railway.

Ashley was five years old when his father died and his future looked bleak. Due to his grandfather being Scottish by birth, he was evacuated once more, with his family, to an army camp at Bridge of Weir in Scotland. Treated as war refugees, they lived in draughty Nissen huts in poor conditions. He was sent to a local school, which he hated, but whilst playing truant, Ashley found that the inspiring scenery gave him his first urge to create pictures. His schoolbooks were put to a new use, as sketchpads. On his birthday he demanded a paint box and began to colour in his sketches.

After two years of misery, his maternal grandfather obtained their release and booked passage for them on a ship bound for Penang. They returned to their former home in a state of euphoria, revelling in the tropical sunshine and grateful to enjoy exotic food and fruits again instead of the porridge, boiled beef and stewed

The Scott family – Left to Right – a family friend (Scottish),
Ashley (aged 6), Uncle Clive, Grandma Claudia, Ashley's Mother.

cabbage of the refugee camp. Grandpa Scott found his mansion relatively intact. It was sorely in need of maintenance and over-run with lizards, but quite habitable.

The situation in Singapore was much worse, for the life that they had left behind no longer existed. Both family houses had been raised to the ground and their servants massacred by the Japanese. Their possessions had disappeared and all the companies in which they held shares had been terminated.

Ashley remained in Penang and enjoyed one of the best periods of his childhood. Nearby relatives owned a rubber plantation and a stable full of horses. Weekends were spent riding through the trees and ripping off the fresh rubber as it oozed down their trunks into bowls.

Another pastime was snake hunting, but this activity was curtailed after a particularly hair-raising episode in which Ashley, who had been tied to a tree, was confronted with an inquisitive snake that slithered around his feet. His playmates managed to chase it away with sticks, but from thereon Ashley's enthusiasm for the sport quickly waned.

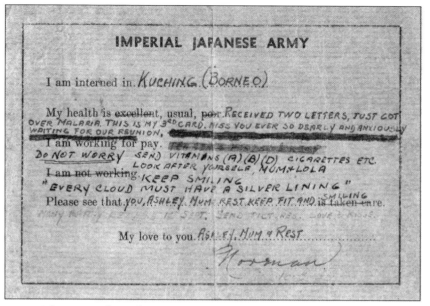

A letter sent from the Japanese concentration camp in Borneo where Norman Jackson was interned and later died.

School was still a problem and his performance continued to be poor. In addition Ashley's conduct deteriorated and he became a rebellious and spoiled brat. Things came to a head when he stole some lead soldiers that his grandfather had painstakingly dressed in biblical clothes in order to create a Nativity scene. When the theft was discovered his grandfather was so angry, he spent a whole day interrogating his servants. Ashley was persuaded to confess and when he reluctantly did so the effect was devastating. His grandfather was reduced to tears, declaring that he had been humiliated in front of his servants. A penitent Ashley was made to apologise to each servant and ask for forgiveness.

Shortly afterwards Ashley was sent to his mother in Singapore, who was not pleased to see him. He arrived at an inopportune time, for her life, and subsequently his, was about to undergo a dramatic change. She had formed a relationship with a British serviceman, Hedley Haigh, who had chosen to remain in Singapore when the war ended, and Ashley was packed off to boarding school. The experience was hellish and thankfully short-lived. Desperately unhappy, he was moved to a day school in Kuala Lumpur where he was the sole European and still bottom of the class

His mother married Hedley and the three of them sailed for England on the SS *Canton*, which began a new chapter in his life. They settled in Linthwaite, a village to the south-west of Huddersfield and their home was a small terraced house in Hazel Grove. It was here that Ashley began his lasting love affair with Yorkshire and its rugged Pennine moors that clasped him to their heart. He marvelled at their sense of atmosphere and wild beauty. He grew to love Yorkshire people and their forthrightness. 'What you see is what you get,' sums them up in Ashley's view. In his opinion they share the gritty qualities of the moors that surround them.

The thing that most affected Ashley immediately after his move to England was the sight of white people performing menial tasks, which were carried out by the indigenous population in Malaya. To see white men lifting dustbins, sweeping the streets and opening hotel doors came as a shock to an impressionable boy.

It was not long before the family moved to Barnsley, where Ashley began to place his roots. At his new school he adopted the name Norman, because in the playground, a name such as Ashley would have brought ridicule and branded him a sissy. Eventually his confidence grew thanks to some good and friendly teachers. Art became his saving grace. Miss Netherwood, his art teacher nurtured his painting skills and wherever Ashley went he took his sketchbook with him.

However, his home life was not so happy, because he had an unfortunate relationship with his domineering step-father, who was extremely strict.

The embryonic signs of success were beginning to manifest themselves when Ashley won first prize in an art competition on the theme of Road Safety. He became a school prefect, his first position of responsibility, and eventually was appointed Head Boy.

At the age of fifteen he enrolled at Barnsley School of Art and during his time there he searched for employment so that he was not beholden to his father for his keep. He applied to Ron Darwent, a greatly respected local sign-writer, for an apprenticeship in sign-writing and glass gilding. Initially Ron turned him down indicating that at the age of seventeen Ashley was too old.

Working as a sign-writer

Muker Show

Undaunted, Ashley pestered him until he relented and gave him the biggest break of his life. He learnt skills that have served him admirably throughout his artistic career. The intricacy of lettering on various materials, including glass, the hardest medium to master, provided an invaluable challenge to the aspiring craftsman. Ashley's only drawback during this exciting learning period was his poor spelling, which resulted in several unfortunate incidents.

Ron became a father to Ashley through his unstinting guidance, encouragement and companionship. The benevolent sign-writer introduced him to the beauty of the Yorkshire Dales by way of frequent camping trips. He was taken to remote and spectacular regions where he marvelled at the enormity of the landscapes and their sullen beauty. His love of walking was also fostered during those excursions and he developed an acute sensitivity to the wind and rain that lashed the exposed higher reaches of his newly discovered world. The fresh tang of saturated heather and rain-

Ashley's art shop in Barnsley, now enlarged into a gallery.

soaked leafy glades tantalised his nostrils.

Ashley particularly enjoyed their visits to Swaledale, particularly the area comprising the Swale Gorge and the localities of Muker, Thwaite and Keld. It still remains a firm favourite. 'By Keld's gold stream' is an apt description in Ashley's view and its tumbling waterfalls, such as Kisdon Force inspired him and he likened them to torrents of Tetley's bitter.

A firm bond developed between master and pupil, particularly through those early camping expeditions, and Ron was later to become best man at Ashley's wedding. Their friendship has endured through the years and they can be frequently found walking the moors together.

As Ashley's eighteenth birthday approached, girls were unapproachable beings as far as he was concerned. He had no real girlfriend and had to be content with his adolescent fantasies. All this changed suddenly when a model turned up for a Fine Art class at Barnsley School of Art. To Ashley's amazement she completely disrobed. He was mesmerised and unable to concentrate on painting. Dissolving into fits of nervous laughter, he was dismissed from the class and ordered to paint the Art School gates as punishment.

This humiliation, however, turned into a wonderful opportunity, because through those gates walked an attractive fifteen year old girl, who was attending a commerce class in the Art School annex. Her effect on Ashley was stunning and he could not take his eyes off her.

He stretched out the gate painting three times longer than it should have taken, in order to catch another glimpse of the beautiful apparition. When she passed him once more, his lovelorn glances made no impression and he was frustratingly ignored.

Racking his brains for an excuse to meet her Ashley drew a blank, but he discovered that her name was Anne Hutchinson. He was beginning to think that she would remain an intangible treasure when fate intervened. She unexpectedly attended a reunion dance organised by Holyrood School for its former pupils. Luckily Ashley was a decent dancer and he never left her side all that evening. Thus began a five-year courtship that culminated in their marriage. Money was hard to come by in those days and they were determined not to wed until they could afford to.

Their marriage was worth the long wait, for they have enjoyed thirty-seven years together and raised a wonderful family that Ashley cares passionately about. They have two children and four grandchildren. Their daughters are named Heather, after moorland heather and Claudia, after his maternal grandmother. Each daughter has two children and Ashley contends that his greatest achievement, far greater than having his paintings exhibited, is seeing his young grandchildren.

Having experienced so much death during his early life has taught him to appreciate, not only the blessing of a family, but also how providential his life has been. This has resulted in an awareness of people less fortunate than himself and his acknowledgement that 'there but for the grace of God go I.' He has spent ten years of his life teaching art at Wakefield Prison and does a great deal of charity work in order to repay a little of what fate has bestowed on him.

On their return from honeymoon Ashley and Anne set up home

Gunnerside Gill, Swaledale

The Swale Gorge

West Tanfield

Ashley's impression of Wycliffe, near Barnard Castle

in New Street, Dodworth, a mining village on the outskirts of Barnsley. The district is known locally as 'Top of Dodworth Bottom.' There was no bathroom in the compact terraced house and the outside toilet was shared with three other families. Despite these drawbacks they were proud of it and happy to live there.

Anne was responsible for what Ashley considers the most important painting that he has produced. After their honeymoon he got out the sketch that he had made on their first date, when she had accompanied him to the hills near Stocksbridge, chaperoned by her younger sister. He had drawn a derelict cottage in the broad sweep of the Ewden Valley, on that occasion. When he finally completed the painting, to please and impress his young bride, he knew that it was different to his other work. The mood was darker, more thoughtful and almost sombre. For the very first time Ashley had depicted the desolation and echoing emptiness of the moors.

That painting represented the initial step along the artistic road that he was destined to follow. It was highly commended by two respected authorities of the Barnsley Art Society and Ashley, thus encouraged, began to devote all his spare time to painting. He also joined the Society and reverted to his real christian name, on the grounds that it sounded more artistic. Gradually he built up a large portfolio and the *Barnsley Chronicle* showed an interest, printing articles concerning the local lad who specialised in painting the Pennine moors.

At that time he was still a sign-writer by day and if he was going to make it as an artist, he would have to persuade someone to let him stage a one-man exhibition. This was finally achieved in 1965 when he was allowed to exhibit, at what was really a wine and cheese party to raise funds for the Liberal Association, in Brighouse. Out of the twelve paintings on show, Ashley sold six, which so impressed the organisers that they offered him a full-scale exhibition, less than three weeks later.

He gathered together thirty-six watercolours and designed an enormous poster to hang outside the Liberal headquarters, a distinctive building in Bethel Street, Brighouse. It read, 'Ashley Jackson Exhibition. Pay Nowt to Come In!' Two hundred people, unable to resist 'summat for nowt,' turned up and twelve paintings were sold. In addition he received nine commissions and for the first time he was paid more than one pound for a painting.

Ashley with the then Prime Minister, Harold Wilson.

Partially helped by publicity, interest in his work began to spread, even beyond the Yorkshire boundary. His paintings sold steadily, if not spectacularly and Ashley took the gamble of acquiring his first premises, in order to build up a studio-cum-gallery.

Unfortunately this meant splitting from his friend and mentor, Ron Darwent. It was an emotional occasion for Ashley when he finally plucked up the courage to tell him. Surprisingly, but like a true friend, Ron took it calmly and with compassion, listening attentively to Ashley's plans. He agreed to every proposal and even allowed Ashley to continue sign-writing to help his survival.

Two months after the opening of his studio Ashley was offered another one-man exhibition, a real one, which lasted for two whole weeks. To his delight he sold every one of his paintings, worked from shivering sketching sessions along the rain-swept Buttertubs Pass, amidst the misty heights of Wensleydale and Arkengarthdale and the remote area surrounding the Tan Hill Inn.

Ashley at work in the Yorkshire Dales

Spurred on by this success, Ashley submitted three paintings to the Royal Academy, which were promptly thrown out. Undeterred, he decided to stage his own exhibition in the capital, alongside pavement artists on the Embankment. As luck would have it England were playing in the World Cup Final that weekend and the streets were full of jostling people, many of whom stopped to examine his paintings.

His biggest break, however, appeared in the form of a BBC film crew, which attracted an even greater crowd. Public exposure on national television was more than he had ever dared to expect.

After a further three years of struggle, 1969 proved to be a golden year for Ashley. His eldest daughter, Heather was born, which seemed to set in motion a fantastic train of events.

Whilst exhibiting his paintings in Dewsbury, a grey-haired old man wandered into the room and began to inspect his work very closely. Ashley immediately recognised the distinguished figure of James L. Brook, one of the art world's elder statesmen. He was an acknowledged authority and critic and when he spoke, everyone listened.

To Ashley's amazement he spoke of his work in glowing terms, indicating that never before had he seen such broad, confident washes from a young artist. He urged him to carry on painting in that manner, to the exclusion of all else. His glowing praise had a galvanising effect on Ashley, who was more determined than ever to break into the art stratosphere represented by London.

He trailed around one London gallery after another until one curator offered to show some of his paintings to its governors. On the strength of these he was offered his own exhibition for the staggering period of two and a half weeks.

Never one to fight shy of publicity, Ashley took the opportunity to inform the Press, which resulted in his name appearing in the national newspapers, including the *Times.* This exposure alerted the critics, who turned up in force and luckily, liked what they saw.

Later that year another glorious event took place. It came about because James L. Brook was a friend of L.S. Lowry and he must have mentioned Ashley's name to the revered artist.

One morning, out of the blue, Lowry walked into Ashley's gallery. Stupefied, the young artist blurted out some sycophantic remark, to which the great man replied, 'Nay lad, nay! I'm only human.'

Not to Ashley, he wasn't. He was the North's supreme artist of the century and he was actually in his gallery. 'Do you hear sir? Only human!' Lowry repeated.

Lowry addressed everyone as 'sir' and the word jerked Ashley out of his stupor. He waited in torment for the judgement of Solomon as the old man proceeded to inspect his paintings. He need not have worried. 'I take my hat off to you sir,' proclaimed Lowry. 'Indeed, I will take it off to any good water colourist, and you are one of the finest there is sir!' As those words began to penetrate, Ashley was further astonished by the great artist's decision to purchase one of his paintings.

Before he left, Lowry gave Ashley his address and telephone number, saying that he could call and see him at any time if he needed advice. Ashley took him up on the offer and visited Lowry's home at Mottram, Longdendale, on many occasions. They became firm friends and Ashley became aware of his idol's amazing judgement and humility. One of the most touching stories, of the many that Lowry related, reflected his love of children. It concerned the occasion when he was painting a cricket match and a nine-year-old girl, who lived near to him, turned up and watched his progress. At the time, he was painting a clump of trees behind the pavilion when she exclaimed, 'Mr Lowry! What are you doing? You know you can't paint trees.'

'Oh,' said Lowry. 'What should I do then?' 'Put in some mill chimneys instead, of course!' 'She was absolutely right,' Lowry told Ashley. ' I did just that and it worked a treat.'

That wonderful year of 1969 was a launching pad and Ashley went from strength to strength. After Lowry's untimely death he was asked to do an interview about his friend for Yorkshire Television. This led to a resident spot on *Pebble Mill at One*, working alongside Donny MacLeod and Jan Leeming. That programme brought national exposure every week and people began to stare at him whilst he was doing his indispensable sign-writing. They would say, 'Hey lad. I've just seen thee on television. What the 'ell are you doing up that ladder!'

His financial worries at last began to ease and his paintings became well recognised. The rest, as they say, is history, and Ashley's reputation and stature as an artist continued to grow. He made many more television appearances and achieved international artistic recognition. Many will recall his highly successful series for Yorkshire Television, such as *A Brush with Ashley* and *Ashley Jackson's World of Art*. He has also written four very successful books, including an autobiography entitled *My Brush with Fortune*.

Although his artistic skill is world-renowned and he is asked to make frequent lectures abroad, he is always conscious of his roots. Though he is not a Yorkshireman by birth, he always 'bats for Yorkshire' throughout his lectures. The county and its people have made him what he is today and he represents them with a true passion. He maintains that it is humour and passion that make Yorkshire such a great county.

At the present time, Ashley is as busy as ever. He normally paints between September and March, for he likes the more vivid and climatic landscapes of autumn and winter. People who watch him

An Ashley Jackson sketch

paint his watercolours marvel at the speed with which he works. Some accuse him of undue haste, but others who know better realise that the faster an original idea takes shape the purer it becomes. This skill was acquired during the time that he spent amongst the working-class people of Kualar Lumpur, where he learned to handle a Chinese brush pen with speed and dexterity. He also learned to cope with fewer material benefits and cultivated an agreeable amount of independence and resourcefulness.

It is these qualities that have made Ashley go his own way in life. He refuses to bow to political correctness or diplomacy and has little belief in the art establishment, who brand him a popularist. Ashley is used to such reproach, for throughout his artistic life he has been criticised for specialising in topographical landscapes. Experts deem him predictable, but he counters this with his own view of an expert. He is indebted in this respect to his hero, Blaster Bates, the Cheshire demolition engineer, who would never describe himself as such. His cryptic definition of the word was 'ex' stands

An Ashley Jackson sketch

for 'has been' and 'spert' means 'a drip under pressure.'

For the remainder of the year, when he is not painting, Ashley exhibits his work in order to make a living. If he were rich enough he would not sell any of his original paintings and he has always loathed parting with them. The greatest accolade, in his eyes, is when ordinary folk show an interest in his work, for he believes that art should not be elitist and should be enjoyed by everyone.

Another of his maxims is 'practice makes perfect.' For every painting Ashley exhibits, a further six or seven are destroyed, such is his devotion to excellence. He also believes that the fiercest critic of your work should be yourself and you must learn to observe it with impartiality. In his opinion many people look at a painting but don't see its true meaning.

Ashley has many projects in the pipeline, not least being an exhibition, covering the complete spectrum of his artistic career, at the Royal Armouries in Leeds. It will take place from May to

September next year and is in recognition of his reaching the age of sixty.

He is also working on another book, to be published in May 2000, which will feature sixty colour illustrations of his paintings, to represent the sixty years of his life, and a number of his sketches.

Television commitments include a series for Yorkshire Television, starting in December of this year, entitled *Your Favourite View,* which will also be shown on the Discovery Channel. He will also be working on another project, in the form of a documentary about his life that will include excerpts from his previous television appearances.

On the evidence of the above Ashley will not be relaxing, or reaching for the pipe and slippers, for some time to come. He has no intention of giving up the profession that he loves and when his time is finally over and he enters the pearly gates, he will probably say to St Peter, 'Ere, can I have a brush and some paint and are there any moors up here?'

CHAPTER EIGHT
The Redoubtable Lady

Lady Anne Clifford was a fine advertisement for feminism, for she struggled to overcome the male chauvinism of her day that prevented her inheritance of the family estates until she was well into her fifties.

A person of great resolve and fortitude, she spent so much of her life fighting against seemingly impossible odds that it is not surprising that the force of her personality is felt today. Throughout the Yorkshire Dales and Eden, people speak of Lady Anne as someone ever-present, so strongly is her influence perceived in the area.

She was born in 1590, within the impressive precincts of Skipton Castle. At that time the family estates covered a large proportion of the Yorkshire Dales and part of Cumberland and Westmorland, an extensive feudal empire amassed by three centuries of noble Clifford stock.

Lady Anne was a studious girl, extremely devoted to her mother, Margaret Russell, daughter of the second Earl of Bedford. They became very close and in her writings, Lady Anne describes her as graceful, courteous, spirited and unyielding to ill-fortune or opposition. Her father, George Clifford, third Earl of Cumberland, was a committed seafarer and accomplished navigator, who took part in the defeat of the Spanish Armada. Unfortunately some of his exploits wasted the estates, by the pouring of money into a series of ill-fated seafaring expeditions.

Educated by her governess, she also enjoyed the tutorage of the poet Samuel Daniel, from whom she acquired an early love of books. Lady Anne was a proficient student of history, poetry and classics. At the age of thirteen, by which time her family had moved to London, she was introduced at court and became a firm favourite of Elizabeth I.

Her father died in 1605 and although only fifteen years old, Lady Anne, as the only direct descendant, had every right to inherit his vast estate. To her astonishment and dismay, she found that he had not entrusted it to her. The Earl of Cumberland could not have

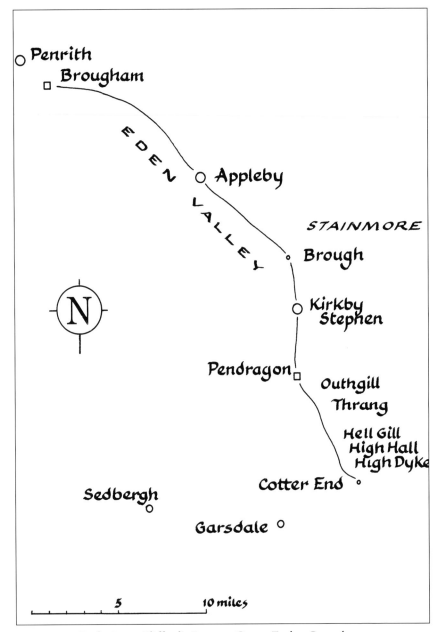

Lady Anne Clifford's Route – Cotter End to Brougham

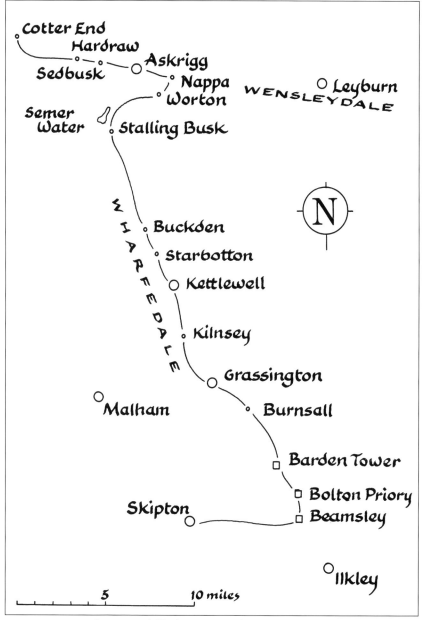

Lady Anne Clifford's Route – Skipton to Cotter End

recognised the strength and determination of his only child, for she was passed over in favour of her uncle, Sir Francis Clifford, who acquired the ownership of the entire family domain.

Almost immediately she and her mother began the struggle to regain the Clifford property. In 1607 they travelled north to the estates and, at the various castles within them, had deeds and other papers referring to their ancestors, copied by secretaries. These later became invaluable sources of information concerning the family and are contained in what Lady Anne described as her 'three great books.'

At the age of nineteen she married Richard Sackville, who, within two days of the marriage became Earl of Dorset. He turned out to be a scoundrel and a playboy, but during the next few years she bore five children, of whom only two daughters survived to adulthood. The earl was also a keen sportsman and a lover of fine clothes, who unfortunately cared little for his wife's claims to her rightful estates. This resulted in a rift between them and on one occasion the earl wrote to Lady Anne, 'Your land transports you beyond yourself.'

When Lady Margaret died in 1617 the dispute concerning the Clifford lands re-surfaced, causing considerable bitterness between Cumberland and Dorset and the king was called upon to arbitrate. Lady Anne was forced to accept the king's verdict, despite her dissatisfaction. Cumberland retained the estates and was obliged to pay Dorset the sum of twenty thousand pounds.

Seven years later, the Earl of Dorset died and, after a further interval of six years, Lady Anne surprisingly married a dissolute and godless widower, Phillip Herbert, Earl of Pembroke. Whether it was a union occasioned by love, or convenience, is open to conjecture, but Lady Anne reputably wrote that it had been wonderfully brought about, by the providence of God, for crossing and disappointing her enemies.

There were two children from the marriage, but sadly they both died in infancy. However, Pembroke provided two valuable assets. Firstly, he employed Indigo Jones to restore the family home of Wilton, thus giving Lady Anne the inspiration for her later building endeavours. Secondly, he provided the name, which she subsequently adopted, of Anne Pembroke. Many of the buildings that she later restored, or built, bear the initials 'AP.'

Only four years elapsed before the marital arguments began, not over the Clifford lands, but over Pembroke's desire to marry one of his sons to Lady Anne's younger daughter. So great was the antagonism that they agreed to live apart.

She continued to live at her husband's houses, Knolle, in Kent and Wilton, in Wiltshire, whilst continuing the battle over her inheritance. She contested ownership, in the courts, of the Clifford estates in 1628 and twice in 1630 without success.

In 1641 her uncle, Francis, Earl of Cumberland, died and her attempt to inherit was again thwarted. The estates passed to his son, much to the annoyance of Lady Anne, but his tenure lasted a mere two years, after which time, he too passed away, without issue.

The opportunity, for which she had waited many years, finally arrived and Lady Anne achieved her prime objective. The enormous Clifford estates and their castles became her rightful property.

Unfortunately the Civil War was in progress and, due to her Royalist sympathies, she was unable to claim her inheritance. It was not until 1649, when the war had ended, that she finally headed north, leaving behind Lord Pembroke, who was to die six months later.

A shock awaited her upon her arrival at Skipton Castle, the ancestral home of the Cliffords, for she found it partially demolished, by order of Parliament. In her eyes this was a desecration of the proud fortification that had protected the family since 1311, when it was granted to Robert, Lord Clifford by Edward II.

Not one to wring her hands in despair, Lady Anne determined that she would not only rebuild the castle, despite Cromwell's threats that he would demolish it, but also the other four in her possession. Although she was nearly sixty years old, her energy, for so long impeded, was now boundless and having had so long to plan her work, nothing could divert her from it.

Thus began a legendary period of refurbishment and travel that was to last until her death in 1676. Lady Anne initiated her famous journeys that took her through her vast estates, which stretched as far north as Penrith. She began regular visits to the castles, or what initially remained of them, of Pendragon, Brougham, Appleby and Brough. Along with Skipton Castle these had suffered badly during the Civil War and were in a perilous state.

Lady Anne, aged thirty, by an unknown artist
(Reproduced by kind permission of Skipton Castle)

The resurrection of these fortifications involved a great deal of cunning, for the spectre of Cromwell and his threats loomed large and such displays of aristocratic wealth were frowned upon in the fledgling republic. Lady Anne was undaunted and began rebuilding in earnest. In addition to the castles, other buildings were restored, or built, including Barden Tower. As a devout Christian, her work encompassed several churches and two almshouses

Travelling by horse-litter, with a large retinue of servants, she embarked on what must have been formidable excursions, over thoroughfares that were often little more than cart tracks, which encompassed the valleys of the Wharfe, Ure, Lune, Eden and Eamont. Lady Anne kept a diary of her journeys, which provides one of the few accounts of the daunting traverse of the inadequate roads and tracks that prevailed in the seventeenth century.

Her first task was to restore her birthplace, Skipton Castle, to its former glory. It had suffered siege by rebels during the Pilgrimage of Grace and she rectified much of the damage inflicted by this

Lady Anne's Highway in the Eden Valley

attack and Cromwell's later demolition.

Amongst the repairs to the castle was the provision of an imposing gateway, which remains to this day. The Clifford family motto 'Desormais,' meaning henceforth, can be clearly discerned above the entrance archway, carved in stone. The original inner doorway, hidden from the exterior, is virtually all that remains of the first Norman castle.

Although Lady Anne made fine work of restoring the castle, she rendered it habitable rather than creating a defensive structure. It does not stand on a well-protected site and resembles a fortified manor house, rather than a castle. Built around a courtyard, it has circular towers at the corners and its warm sandstone walls have mellowed with age to provide a subtle blend of colour and robustness.

Much of the building remains as it was in Lady Anne's time and visitors can tour the Great Hall, kitchens and even the dungeons to obtain an impression of life as it was when the castle was inhabited.

Adjacent to Skipton Castle stands the ancient Holy Trinity Church, its tower dominating the head of the High Street. Lady Anne restored this twelfth-century place of worship in 1655, for it had also suffered considerable damage during the Civil War. She placed new windows in the south aisle and added an array of decorative stonework

The church has long associations with the Cliffords and several members of the family lie within it, in impressive altar tombs. A particularly fine example is the one erected by Lady Anne in memory of her father, which is decorated with heraldry of families connected by marriage to the Cliffords.

When the indomitable Lady Anne embarked on her journeys she travelled in a style appropriate to a prominent member of the aristocracy. She held the office of High Sheriff of Westmorland and the journeys between her properties were conducted in a manner that befits royalty. Her retinue would have numbered around 300 and comprised an extensive travelling train headed by her horse-litter. Ladies-in-waiting and gentlewomen travelled in her coach drawn by six horses; estate officials and menservants were on horseback, her women servants in another coach and all the belongings and equipment were transported by the abundant assembly that followed.

She was determined to live in comfort during her travels and various essential items, such as chairs, tapestries, carpets and curtains were moved from one castle to another to ensure that she maintained an opulent lifestyle.

In addition to staying in her castles, she frequently rested at the home of friends or acquaintances and, anxious to see as much of her estates as possible, she occasionally varied her route.

The first section of Lady Anne's itinerary leads to Beamsley Hospital, a delightful collection of almshouses that stand near the busy A59 Skipton to Harrogate road, approximately seven miles from Skipton. These tasteful, stone-built dwellings were originally intended for poor widows. They were completed by Lady Anne, after initial work by her mother. The unique round chapel forms the centre-piece of the site that is currently in the care of the Landmark Trust, who let the residences as holiday flats.

From Beamsley she travelled through the lands surrounding Bolton Abbey, in upper Wharfedale, to Barden Tower that was

Barden Tower

Mallerstang, in the Eden Valley

Lady Anne's Hospital, Appleby

Brougham Castle

originally built as one of six hunting lodges that lay within the Forest of Barden, the favourite hunting grounds of the Cliffords. The building was enlarged and adapted as a residence in 1485, by Henry, the tenth Lord Clifford, who was known as the 'Shepherd Lord.' He had been raised in a shepherd's family on the Cumberland fells, in order to escape the Wars of the Roses. The Clifford family was Lancastrian and their lands had been confiscated in the war between the two counties. On the accession of Henry VII they were restored and Henry began the conversion of the tower into a home that he was to use for the greater part of his life. He preferred its simplicity to the more opulent Skipton Castle and he found it conducive to his gentle pursuits of astronomy and alchemy. In 1513, at the age of sixty, he commanded a troop at Flodden Field, proving that he also had attributes as a soldier. In some of the farmhouses around Barden there are halberts, which have been passed down to the descendants of men that he led at Flodden.

Lady Anne restored Barden Tower in 1659 and spent many of her final years there. The impressive ruins still display an inscription over the entrance, which indicates that her mother stayed there whilst pregnant with Lady Anne.

The Retainers' House stands opposite the Tower and currently contains a restaurant, in surroundings that are much the same as they were in Lady Anne's time. Mullioned windows and a fine oak roof still remain. A small church adjoins the house, which was repaired by Lady Anne, but subsequently altered during a later restoration in 1860.

Within a mile of Barden Tower stands Hough Mill, originally a soke mill, which was rebuilt by Lady Anne in 1657. It was later used for drying and grinding corn until 1899, when the bursting of the Skyreholme dam swept away a smaller dam that supplied it. The top storey was used at one period by John Lister, the last besom-maker in Wharfedale. It now serves as a barn for an adjoining farm.

On her journeys through the Wharfe valley, Lady Anne stayed overnight at various establishments. Wherever she visited, a stake bed would first be sent and locks were the usual gifts to the host and hostess.

In 1663 she travelled to Rylstone, where she took the old bridle road to Kilnsey and lodged at Kilnsey Hall, which had been built only a few years earlier, in 1648, on the site of Fountains Abbey Grange. Her stay took place during her first journey through Wharfedale to Westmorland and she paid a return visit to the hall on her way back from Mallerstang in 1666.

The delightful village of Starbotton was another of her stopping places, of which she wrote, 'I went to John Symondson's cottage, where I lay one night, and then on to Pendragon, by way of Kettlewell Dale, up Buckden Rakes and over the Stacks into Wensleydale.'

Lady Anne would have found the track up through the Rakes, which follows the Roman route, very rough and stony. This thoroughfare passed the hamlet of Cray, before climbing over the exposed watershed between Wharfedale and Wensleydale. In this wild and blustery landscape she would have traversed Stakes Moss, a desolate, boggy plateau, before descending Cragdale Allotments to Stalling Busk. Here she would have seen the old church near the hamlet, nestling in the deep cleft of Raydale, close to Semerwater. It was built in 1603 and its ruins can still be found in the attractive lakeside setting. A tiny church, built in 1905, has replaced the older version and it stands, within Stalling Busk, on a ridge above the lake.

Her route from Semerwater led to Bainbridge, or Worton, where she forded the River Ure and continued to Nappa Hall, the home of her cousin, Mr. Thomas Metcalfe. It is known that she stayed at this fortified manor house for two nights in 1663. The Metcalfe family continues to have strong associations with the area, particularly Bainbridge, where, by tradition one of its members holds the office of hornblower. The horn is blown at the Rose and Crown Hotel in a ceremony that dates back many centuries. It is performed each evening between the twenty-eighth of September, traditionally the date of Hawes 'Back End Fair,' and 'Pancake Tuesday.' The horn blowing originated as a ritual that called people from the surrounding forest as dusk was falling.

From Nappa she travelled west, climbing above Newbiggin and Askrigg before descending to Sedbusk and Hardraw, the site of the mighty Force that formerly fell a distance of 100 feet before its crest was washed away. It still cascades into a secluded amphitheatre, which is only accessible by passing through the Green Dragon Inn.

A section of this particular route, which passes the hamlet of Helm, is still referred to by the local inhabitants as 'Lady Anne's Road.'

Her course from this point is a little uncertain, but it probably followed the line of what eventually became the Askrigg to Sedburgh turnpike road, for a short distance. This would have brought her to the present junction of Cotterdale Lane and the A684 Hawes to Sedburgh road.

Lady Anne described the next section of her journeys as 'over Cotter and those dangerous ways.' This indicates that she went by a difficult route to the Eden Valley that followed an ancient bridleway, or 'green road.' It began with a steep climb up Cotter Riggs to Cotter End, a prominent hilltop spur, followed by an elevated ride that initially contours Thwaite Bridge Common. This 1500 feet high traverse runs for three miles along a limestone terrace, with bleak moorland above and rough pasture below. Situated beside the track are the remains of High Dyke, which was a drover's inn until the late nineteenth century.

Beyond High Dyke the old 'road' is discernible, threading across grassy slopes above the deserted farmsteads of Shaws and High Way towards the ruins of High Hall. The thoroughfare is known as the High Way and is often referred to as 'Lady Anne's Highway,' for she used it to traverse the testing slopes of the Eden Valley. In addition to suffering the jostling of her horse-litter, she would have been bombarded by the fierce winds that scour the valley and it required a strong constitution to endure the slings and arrows of nature that beset travellers of her era. Despite her discomfort, the visual reward of her surroundings would have provided adequate compensation, because to travel this valley, particularly in winter, is a delight. The bracken-coated fellsides are magnificent; a veritable sea of russet bathed in the glow of a sunken, fragile sun.

On its journey to High Hall the old 'road' passes a lime-kiln, above which is an irregular walled enclosure with a ruined building inside. This was probably a resting-place for packhorses, which provided safe grazing and shelter for the packmen.

Beyond High Hall, Lady Anne would have begun a gradual descent to Mallerstang Common that lies beneath the abrupt slopes of Wild Boar Fell and Hangingstone Scar. During this descent the infant rivers Ure and Eden are crossed. The Ure rises on the dark, spongy slopes of Ure Head, searches out the valley-floor and flows

The Great Picture – Lady Anne aged fifteen and her brothers,
Robert and Francis.
(Reproduction by courtesy of Abbot Hall Art Gallery, Kendal, Cumbria)

southeast towards Moorcock, which lies at the foot of the Eden valley. Within sight of the Moorcock Inn, an ancient hostelry, formerly used by drovers, it turns east and heads for the pleasant market town of Hawes.

Beyond the fledgling Ure, the old road crosses Hell Gill, a dramatic gorge, at the bottom of which flows the infant River Eden. An arched bridge carries the track over the thirty-foot deep ravine

The Great Picture – Lady Anne's parents, George Clifford and
Lady Margaret Russell and Lady Anne, aged fifty-six.
(Reproduction by courtesy of Abbot Hall Art Gallery, Kendal, Cumbria)

and set into its stonework, at the base of a parapet, is an old
boundary stone that marks the division between the old counties of
Yorkshire and Westmorland. Nearby stands a rough stone pillar,
erected in 1664 by Lady Anne to mark the source of the River Eden.
It is inscribed with her initials and is known as 'Lady Anne's Pillar.'

The Eden heads north when it reaches the valley-bottom and

dances with youthful vigour towards Kirkby Stephen. Lady Anne's route crosses it at Thrang, and continues as a walled lane, which is soon replaced by a series of field paths that follow the river to Pendragon Castle.

During this part of the journey, the hamlet of Outhgill, which stands on the opposite side of the river, is passed. The restoration of its church is attributed to Lady Anne and the inscription over the door resembles the one that adorns Barden Tower. It refers to a quotation from Isaiah that reads, 'they that shall be of thee shall build the old waste places.'

Lady Anne fulfilled a childhood dream when she renovated Pendragon Castle in 1663. She and her family spent Christmas in the refurbished fortification, it being the first time for over 100 years that the Cliffords had done so. It is famous for its connection with the legend of King Arthur and it is believed to be the former home of Uther Pendragon, though this is difficult to verify as no trace of a celtic stronghold remains. The name Pendragon was not used until the fourteenth century when Robert de Clifford took advantage of the medieval fascination with Arthurian legend and dispensed with the castle's previous name, Mallerstang, which did not have such popular appeal.

Unfortunately, Lady Anne's successor did not have the same feeling for the castle and promptly plundered it in order to provide a source of dressed stones for his rebuilding at Appleby. However, enough remains of Pendragon to indicate what a stout stronghold it was and one can appreciate its strategic position near the head of the valley, with the Eden swirling around the defensive mound upon which it stands.

The character of the landscape changes as Lady Anne's route heads north from Pendragon towards the Stainmore Gap and her castle at Brough. Rugged high country is left behind for gentler contours, which eventually give way to the desolation of Stainmore.

Her first objective would have been what is now the pleasant market town of Kirkby Stephen. At Pendragon she took another old road, now a stony track that contours the eastern side of Birkett Common on its way to Croop House and the sparse ruins of Lammerside Castle. Indistinct across pastures it eventually joins a farm track leading to the historic fortified house of

Wharton Hall. Here Lady Anne occasionally stayed with the Wharton family, to whom she was related. She usually rested at the hall during her shorter, less taxing travels between Pendragon, Brough, Appleby and Brougham.

Wharton Hall lies within two miles of Kirkby Stephen, the 'capital of the upper Eden,' as it is known. The River has shed its ebullience and becomes more sedate as it discretely glides past the town, seemingly hiding its charms. Although the township lies on an important route to Carlisle it was formerly overshadowed by its neighbour, Brough, whose formidable castle dominates the junction of that route and the well-used A66 road from Scotch Corner that cleaves through the Stainmore Gap. Since Roman times, until the recent past, the A66 road formed part of the main route from London to Scotland and the castle played a major part in its defence.

In recent times, particularly with the coming of the railways, Kirkby Stephen has prospered at the expense of Brough, which, by 1860 was described as little more than a village. It hosts a busy market and lies on one of the most notable long-distance footpaths in the country, Wainwright's Coast to Coast Walk. Many 'Coast to Coasters' make a beeline for its fish and chip shop-cum-restaurant, a mecca for Wainwright devotees since the master of walking guides was shown consuming a healthy portion of fish and chips there during the television series, *Wainwright's Coast to Coast.* In order to perpetuate the legend and to encourage walkers to stop and partake of its delights, the sign outside the shop reads 'Coast to Coast Fish and Chips'

Brough has the feel of a garrison town, which is unsurprising, since it has been associated with armed men throughout its history. The town lies in one of the strategic gaps in the Pennines that has been recognised as an important route throughout the centuries. The Romans built a chain of forts along it, of which Brough was one and later the Normans built their versions on the same sites. Lady Anne inherited the fortification at Brough, whose keep is still known as the 'Roman Tower.' She carried out extensive renovations and these are recalled by the naming of the large round tower on the hall block, 'Clifford's Tower.' She chose to live in this prominence during her visits and had a room at the top of it.

Skipton Castle – engraved by G. Stow from a drawing by N. Whittock (eighteenth century)

During the coaching age, the road over Stainmore was a welcome, though unintentional, provider of victuals to the hard-pressed populace of the area. Accidents or fierce weather often hampered the progress of carts, sometimes causing them to overturn and spill their contents. Word would spread rapidly and in no time the locals would be scavenging for whatever came their way.

In the days before its conversion to part of the modern A66 road, the route from Brough to Appleby and the Eamont Bridge at Brougham was a familiar one to Scottish drovers as they returned from their trips to the English markets. Lady Anne probably followed this drove road on her journeys between the three respective castles.

During the eight-miles traverse from Brough to Appleby, she would have seen the cleft of the Stainmore Gap relent as the valley widens to embrace a maturing River Eden that flows languidly towards Penrith and eventually, the Solway Firth.

Much earlier the Romans marched along this route when moving between their fortifications and in Lady Anne's time the local populace travelled along it to the markets and fairs at Appleby and Brough Hill. These great horse marts were amongst the largest in the country and Appleby Fair still remains an extremely popular

Brough Castle – drawn and engraved by Samuel and Nathaniel Buck (1739)

annual attraction. Events of great character, they attracted gypsies, travellers and visitors, in addition to hordes of local participants.

Appleby bears many examples of Lady Anne's patronage and she describes this attractive former county town of Westmorland as 'the most ancient seat of mine inheritance.' Prior to her rebuilding efforts, the town had suffered greatly at the hands of the marauding Scots, who virtually destroyed it in 1174 and again in 1314. The worst blow occurred in 1388 when the Scots laid the whole town to waste and it did not recover from that devastation for many centuries.

The remnants of the town took another battering at the time of the Civil War, the Royalist sympathies of the Cliffords and the local populace, not endearing it to Cromwell's attacking forces.

Taking its share of the onslaught was the castle, which still proudly dominates the town from its elevated site at the top of Boroughgate, the main thoroughfare. It represents a fitting tribute to Lady Anne's attentions. Probably her finest work was the restoration of the massive Norman keep, which is even larger than the White Tower at the Tower of London. 'The Great Picture,' which she commissioned to commemorate her eventual inheritance of the Clifford estates, is displayed in the Great Hall. This three-panelled picture shows Lady Anne at fifteen, on the death of her father, and at the age of fifty-six. The third panel shows her father, mother and the brothers who died as children.

Under the gaze of the castle gates stands Lady Anne's Hospital, a superb collection of almshouses, set around a cobbled square that houses a shapely fountain. Like many of the buildings in the town these dwellings are constructed from the tasteful local red sandstone and a plaque at the entrance to the cobbled courtyard denotes that they were completed in 1651. Originally twelve widows and 'a mother' lived here and they are still occupied today. Access to the courtyard is permitted, but the adjoining chapel is only open by appointment.

The attractive Church of St Lawrence stands at the foot of Boroughgate, close to the old Moot Hall. Its confines can be described as a shrine to Lady Anne and her mother, who are both buried within. In accordance with the instructions in her will, she lies encased in a lead coffin, bearing a brass inscription, in a vault next to her mother's. She had her vault built shortly after her mother's death and it is decorated with heraldry demonstrating her family tree. It also bears the following caption relating to Lady Anne's death in March 1676, aged eighty-six, 'Christianly, willingly and quietly, havynge before her death seene a plentiful issue by her two daughters of thirteen grandchildren, and her body lyes buryed in this vaulte.'

Lady Anne's rebuilding, which included the Church of St Lawrence, the neighbouring Bongate Church, and her other charitable works, endeared her to the people of Appleby. Despite her generosity she was hard, but fair, in her dealings with her tenants. Her words, 'Retain your loyalty, Preserve your rights,' inscribed on the stone column of the High Cross, which stands outside the castle gates, were both the motto that she lived by and an exhortation to her people.

The final stage of her route, to Brougham, took Lady Anne almost to the northern limit of her vast properties. Throughout her life, she retained a great love and respect for her mother and on the approach to Brougham stands the Countess Pillar, which she erected in her memory. It can be found high on a bank on the south side of the A66 road, marking the place of their final parting before her mother's death in 1617.

Despite being a far-flung outpost of the Clifford estates, Brougham castle was probably her favourite and she restored it with her usual enthusiasm, making it habitable for the first time in many years. A familiar addition, an inscription, on the south wall, details the renovations that she carried out.

Lady Anne also rebuilt the nearby church of St Ninian, which remains, externally, much as she left it. St Wilfred's Chapel also received her attention, the interior of which is decorated with richly carved oak.

During her final years, Lady Anne's family tried to persuade her to restrict her punishing schedule of travel and work, but she remained resilient to the end, declaring that 'she might as well die in her horse-litter as in her bed.'

Brougham Castle was her final resting-place, in its tranquil setting on the bank of the river Eamont. Lady Anne, Countess of Dorset, Pembroke and Montgomery, died in a place that would have satisfied her; the chamber where her father was born and her mother passed away.

She is remembered, not only for her rebuilding and indomitable spirit, but also for her writings and invaluable records. Included amongst these are memoirs of her first husband and various memorials to herself and her ancestors, left in manuscript form.

Appendix

NOTE FOR WALKERS

Reference is made in this book to certain walks and long-distance footpaths, such as the Wolds Way and the Dearne Way. The descriptions of these are not intended as definitive guides. If any of the walks mentioned are undertaken, it is advisable to make use of the relevant Ordnance Survey maps and guide books. The use of weatherproof clothing, boots, or sturdy shoes, is also recommended.

Index